Felix Vallotton

Edited by Lacey Belinda Smith

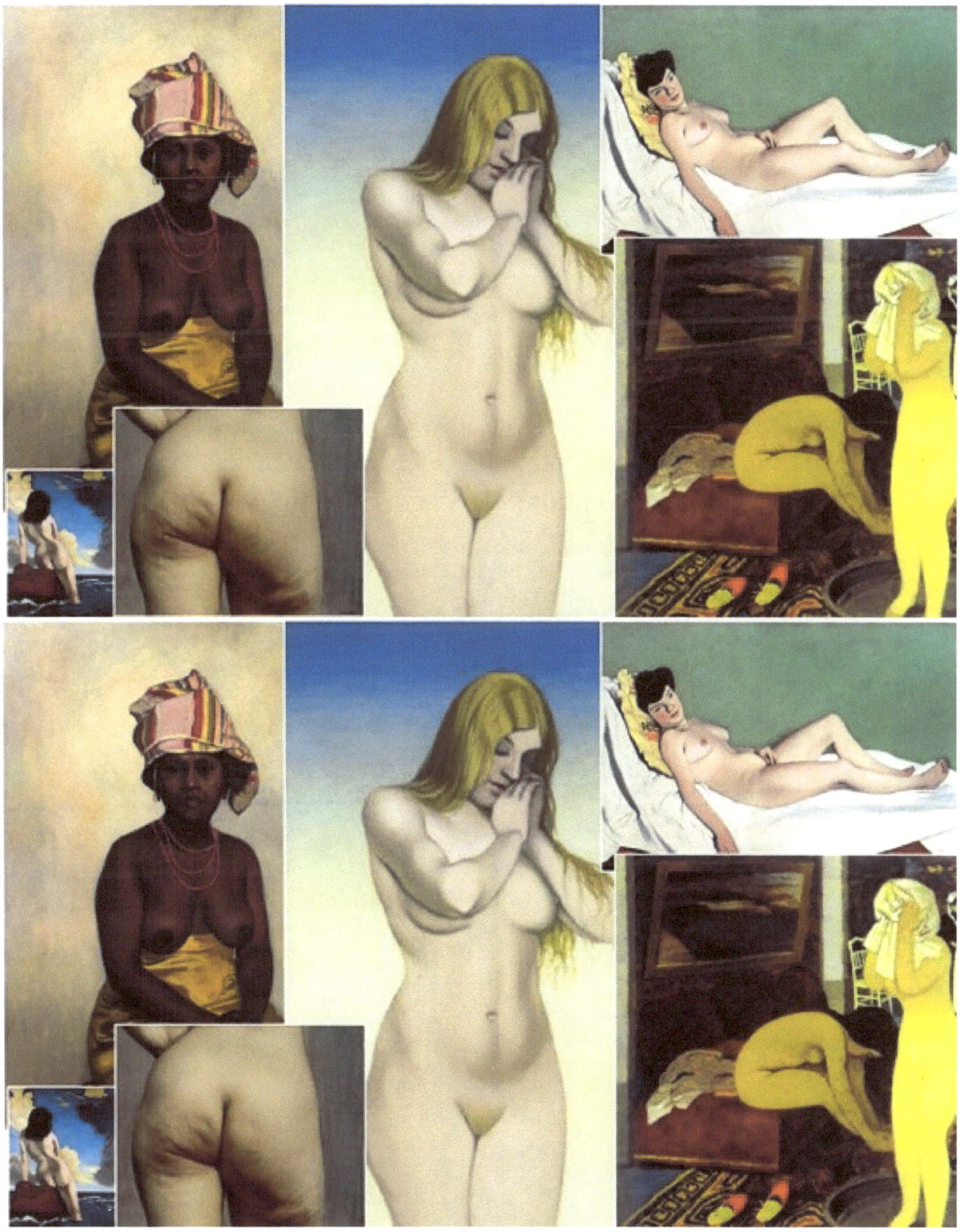

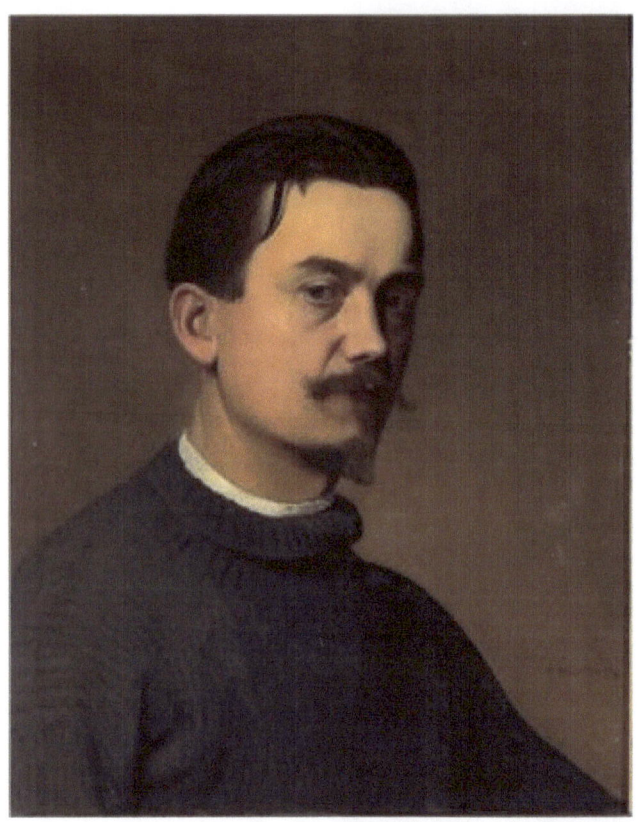

Born in Lausanne, Switzerland in 1865 and obtaining French citizenship in 1900, Felix Vallotton drew his inspiration from this double culture. He died 1925 in Paris, France.

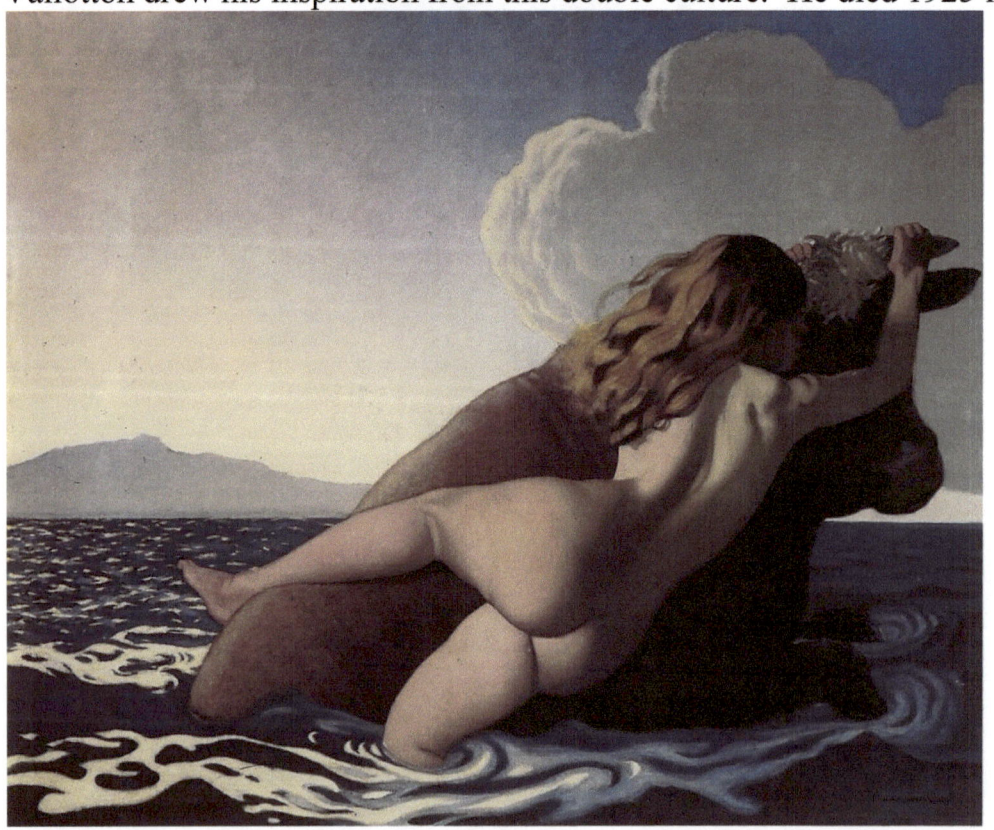

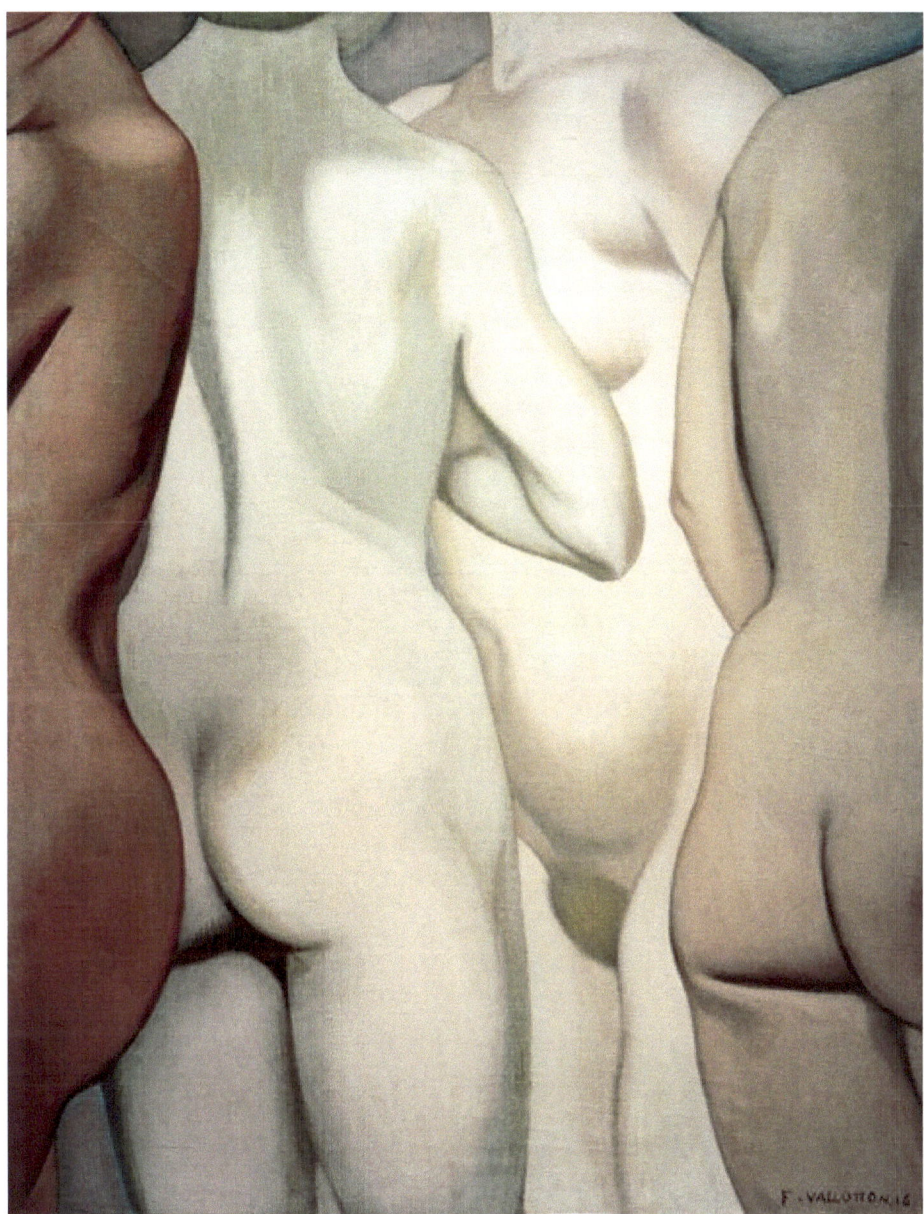

Vier Torsi

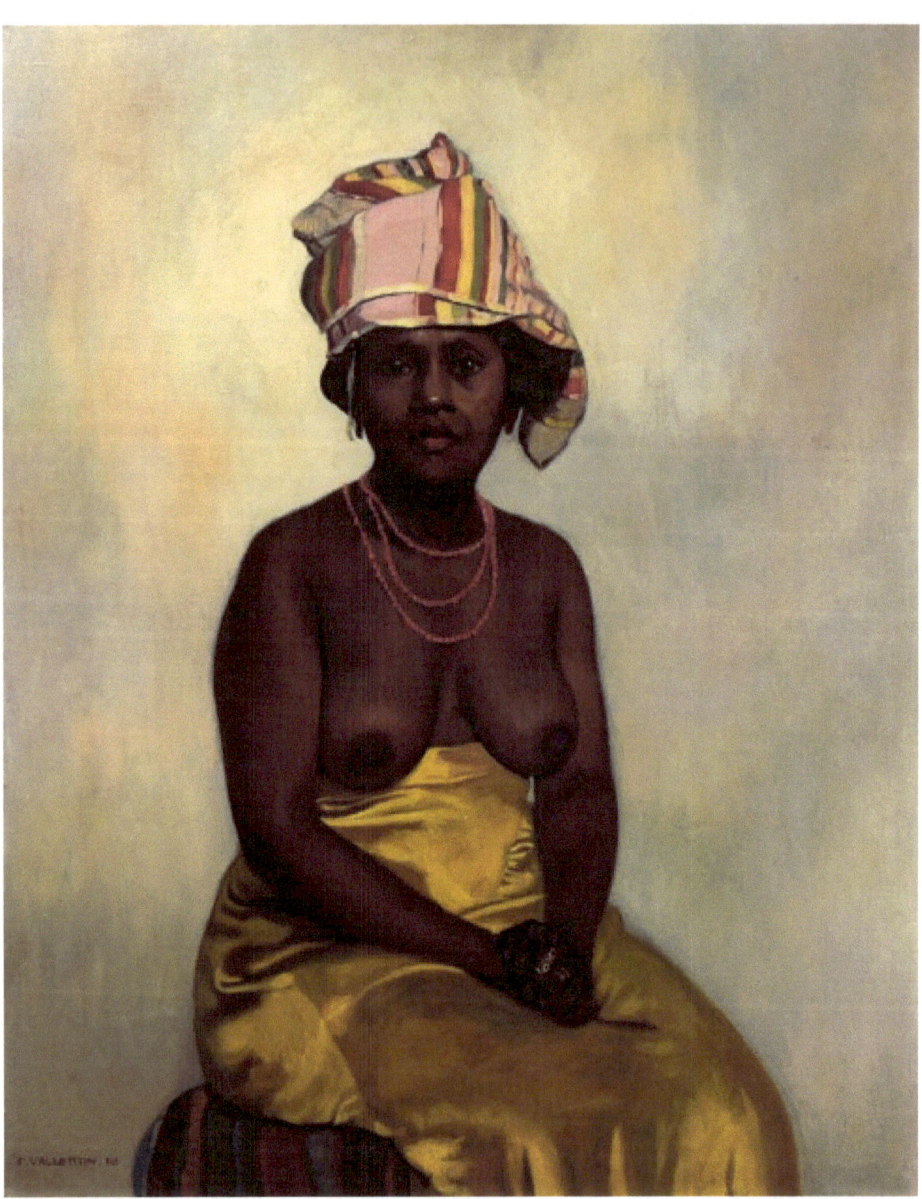

African Woman

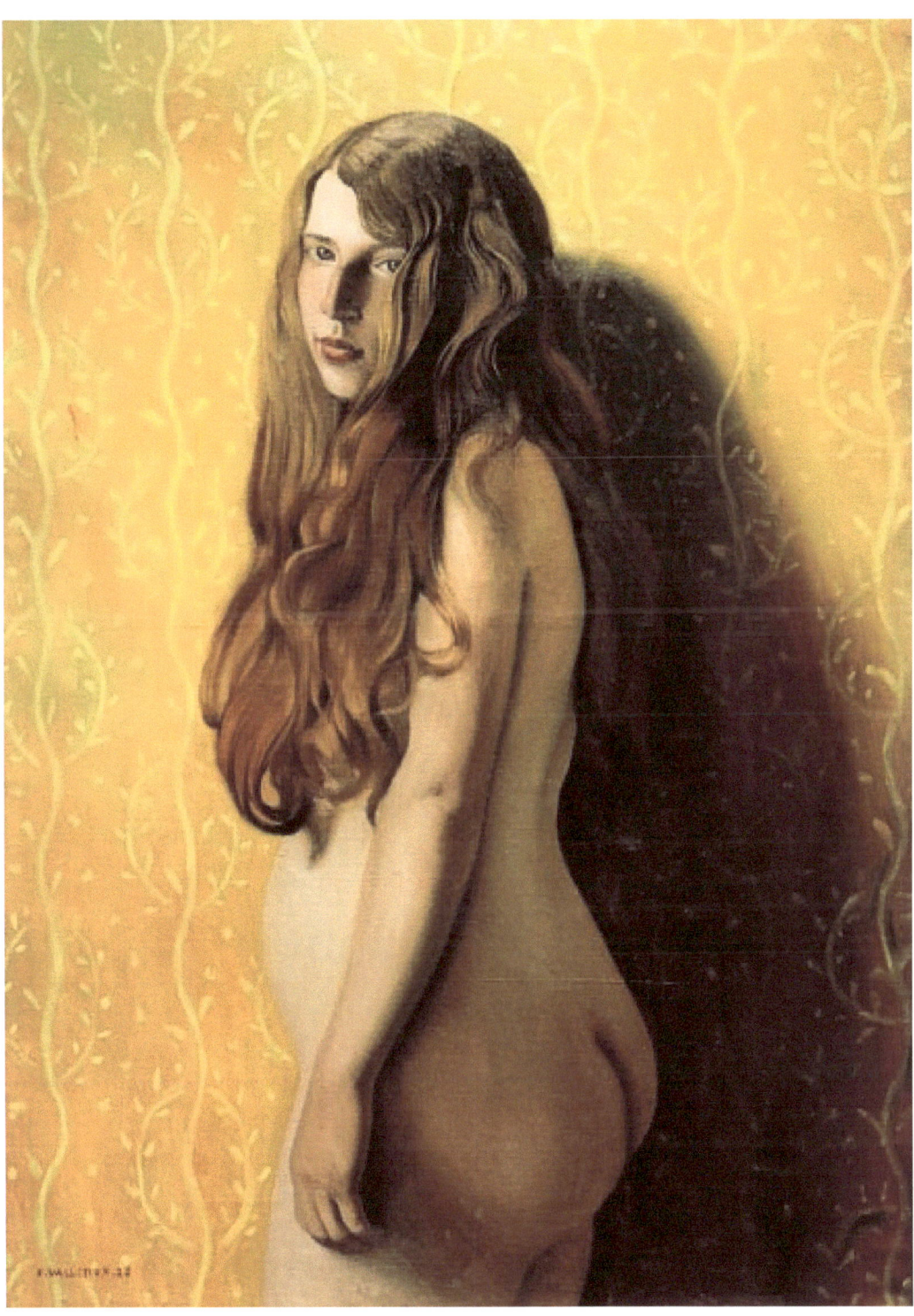

Akt vor gelbem Grund

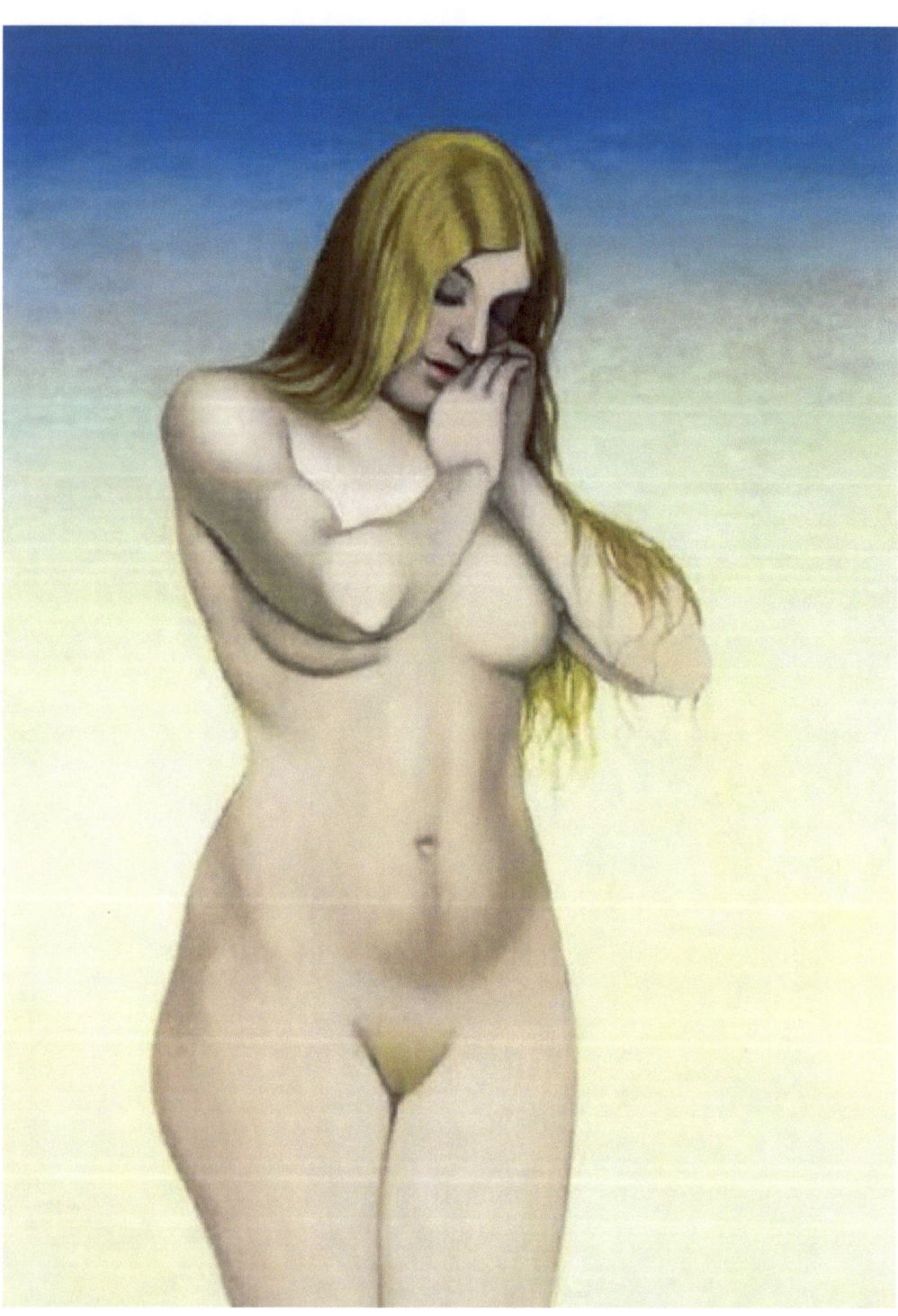

Nu blond

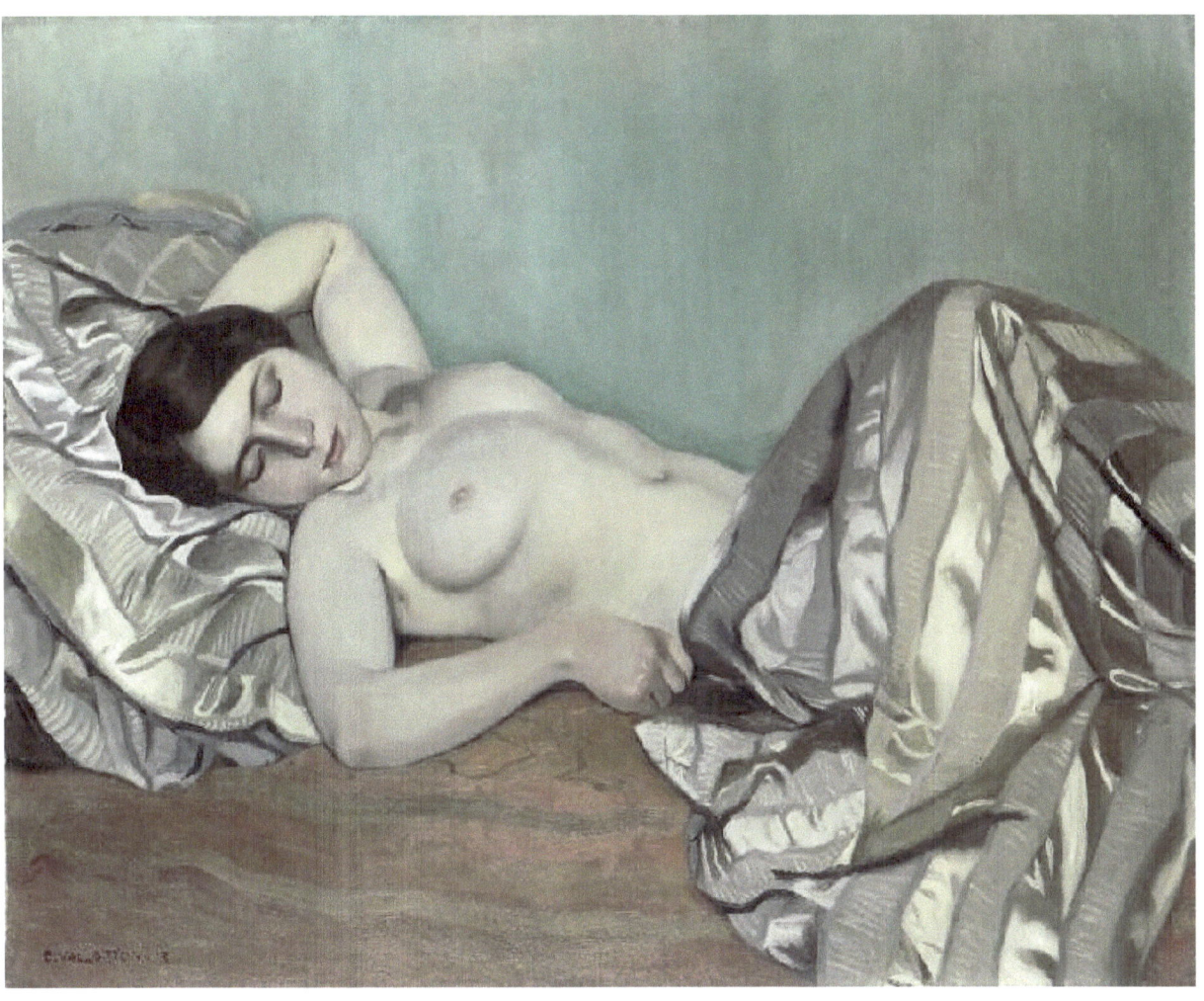

Liegender Halbakt

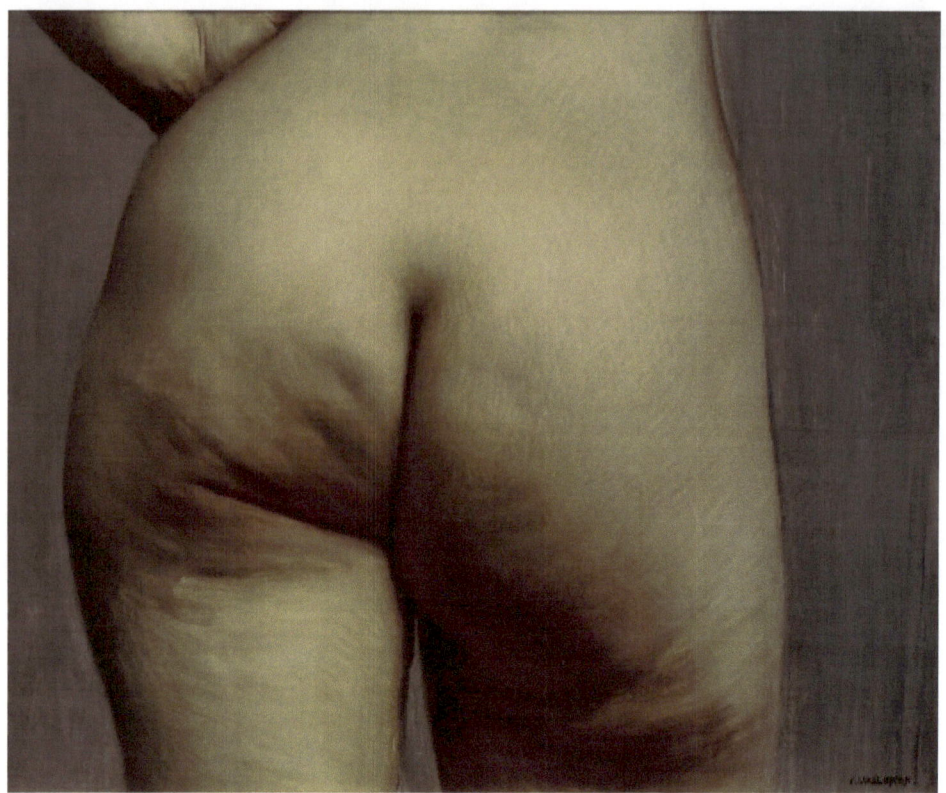

F.Vallotton, Gesässstudie

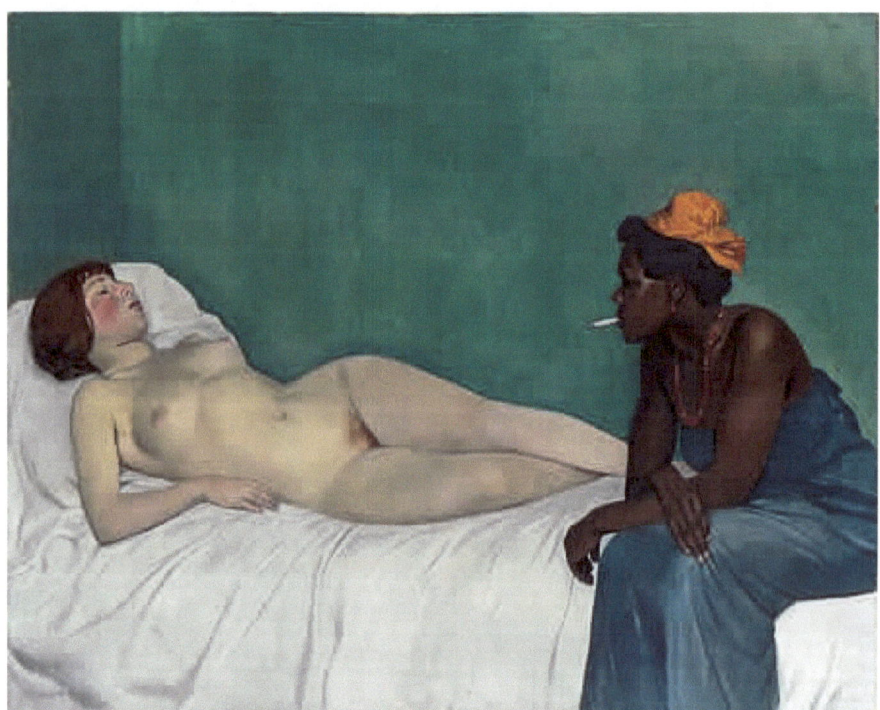

La Blanche et la Noire, 1913

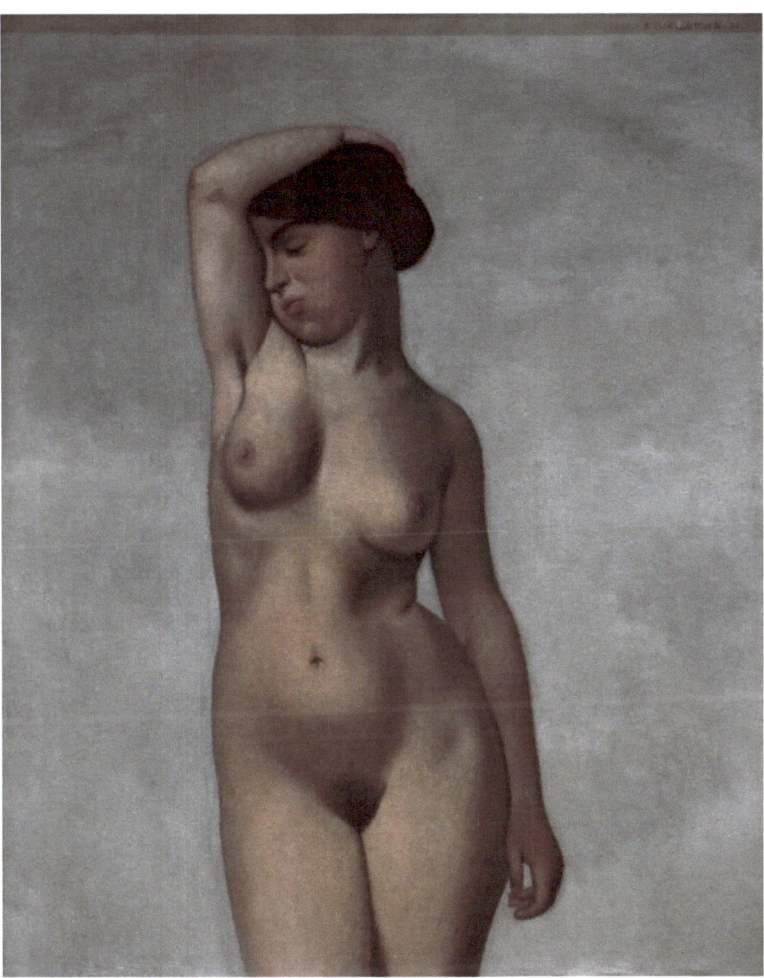

Female nude with raised arm

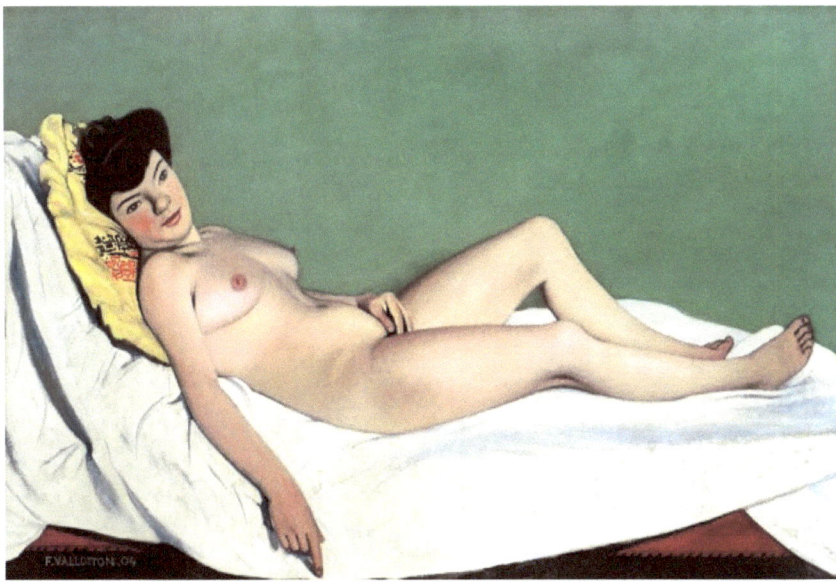

Reclining Nude-- 1904

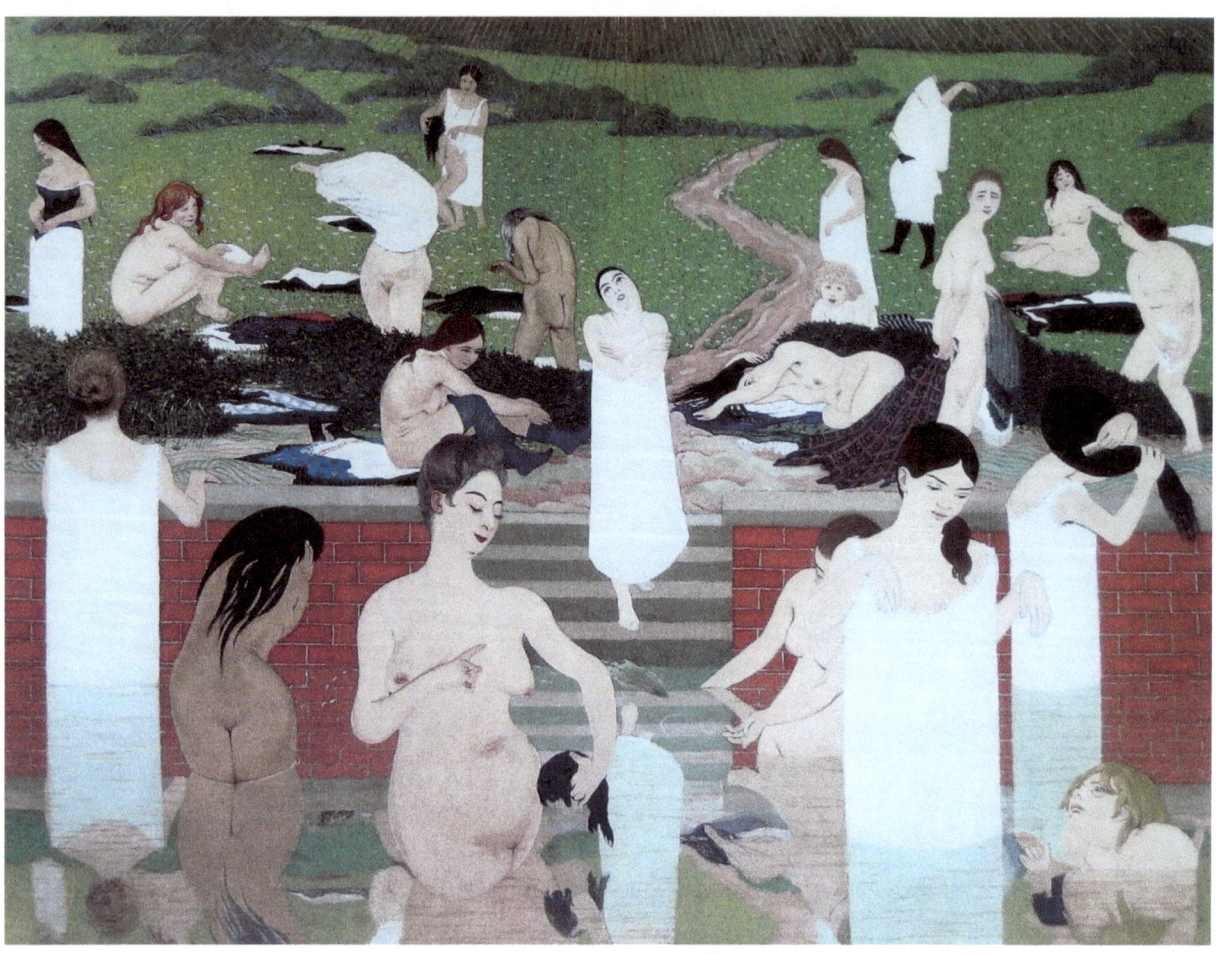

The Bath, Summer Evening, 1892, Post-Impressionism

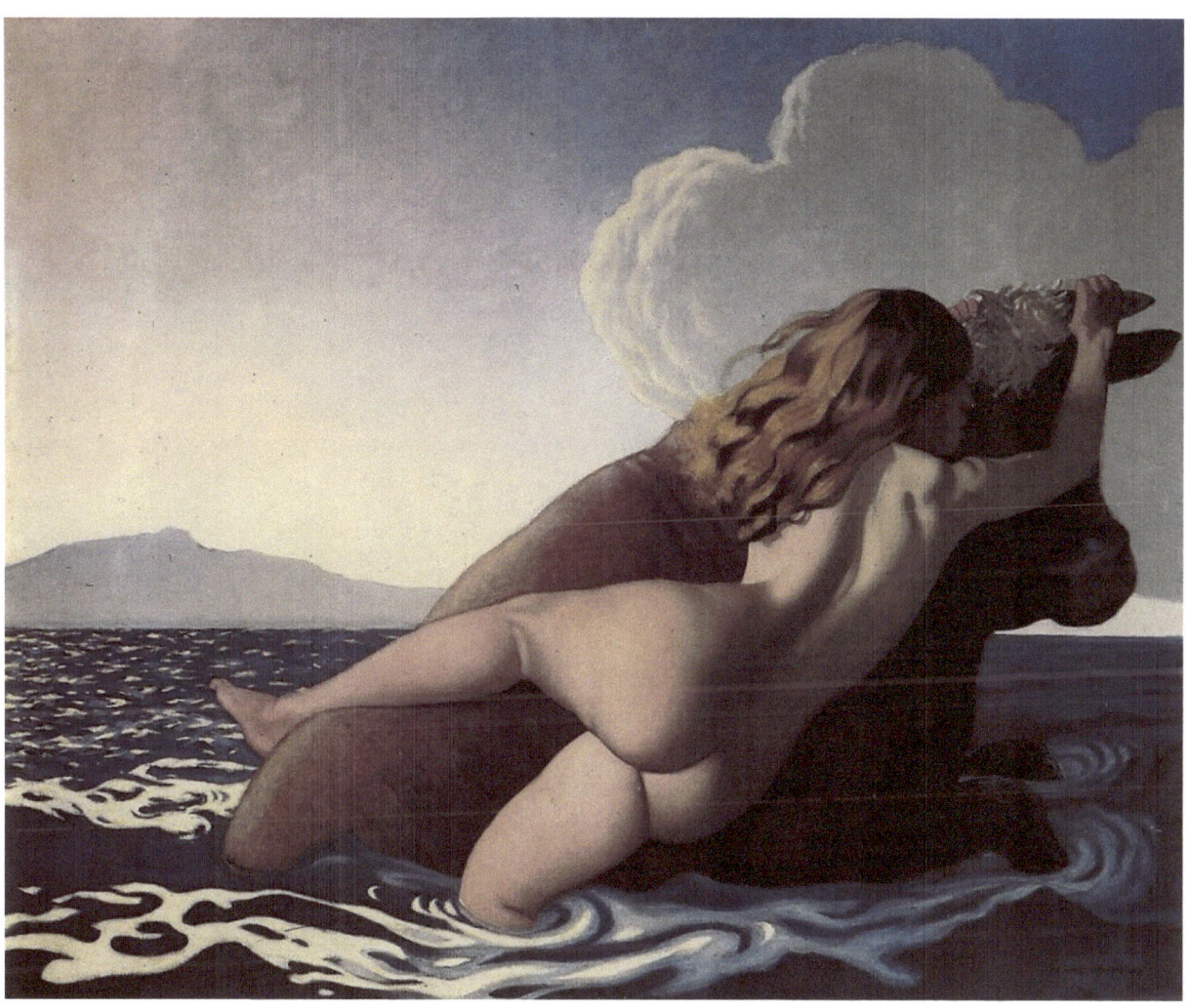

The Rape of Europa, 1908, Magic Realism

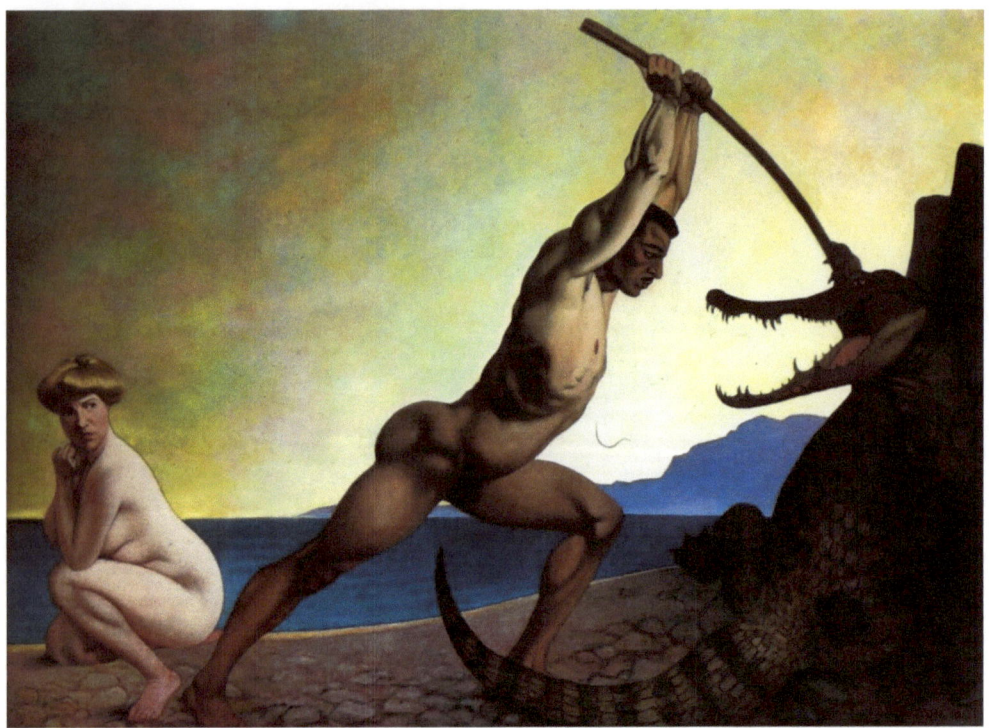

Persee killing the Dragon, 1910, Magic Realism, Genre: mythological painting

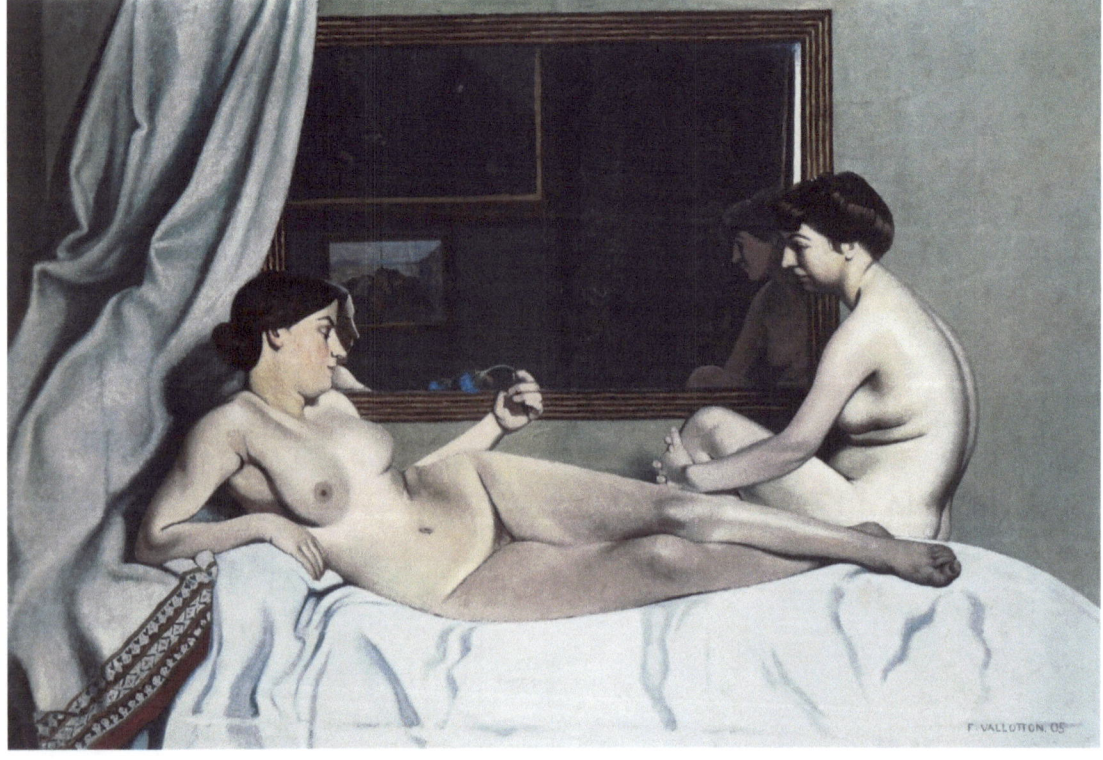

The rest of the models, 1905, Magic Realism

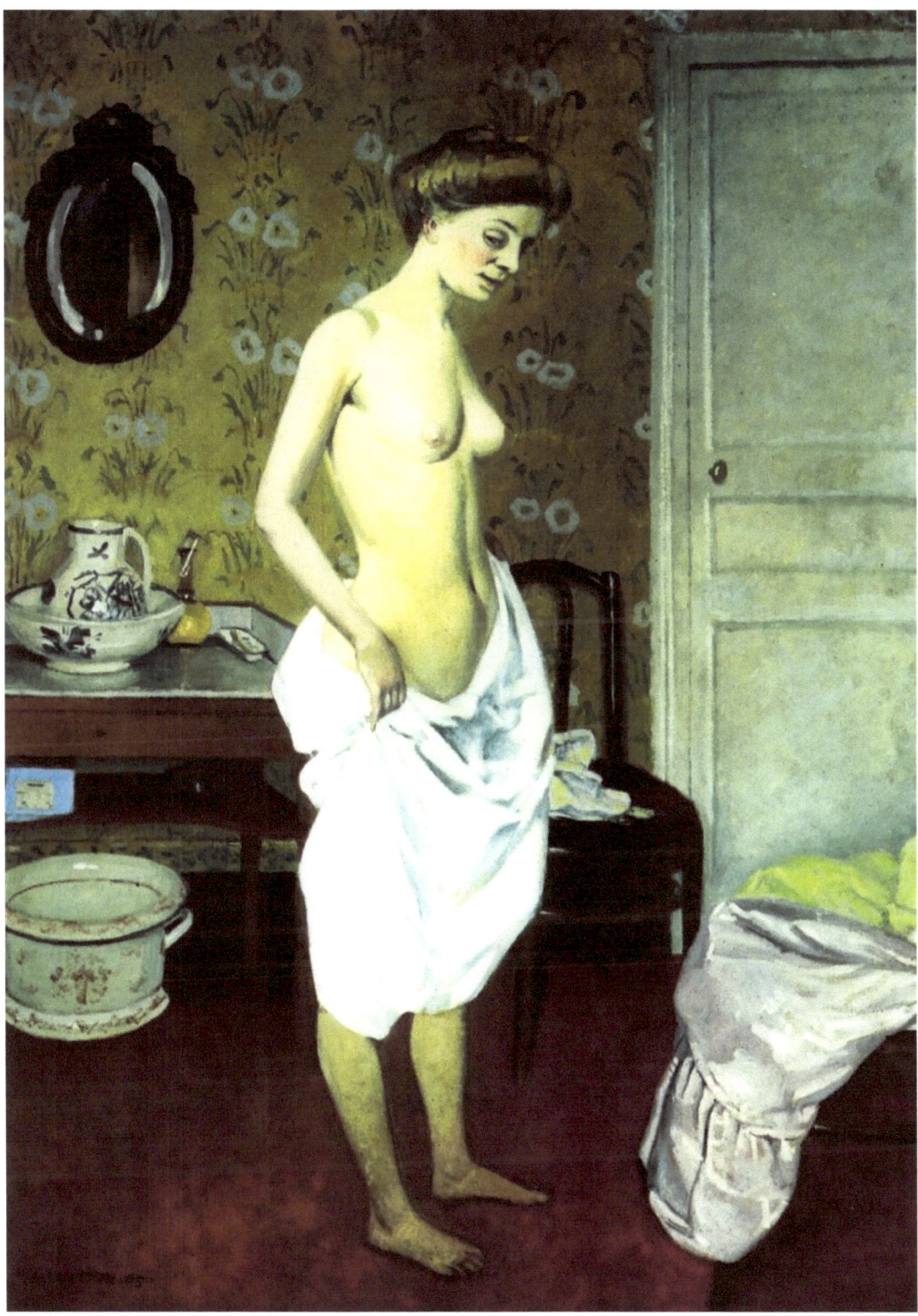

The Toilet, 1905, Magic Realism

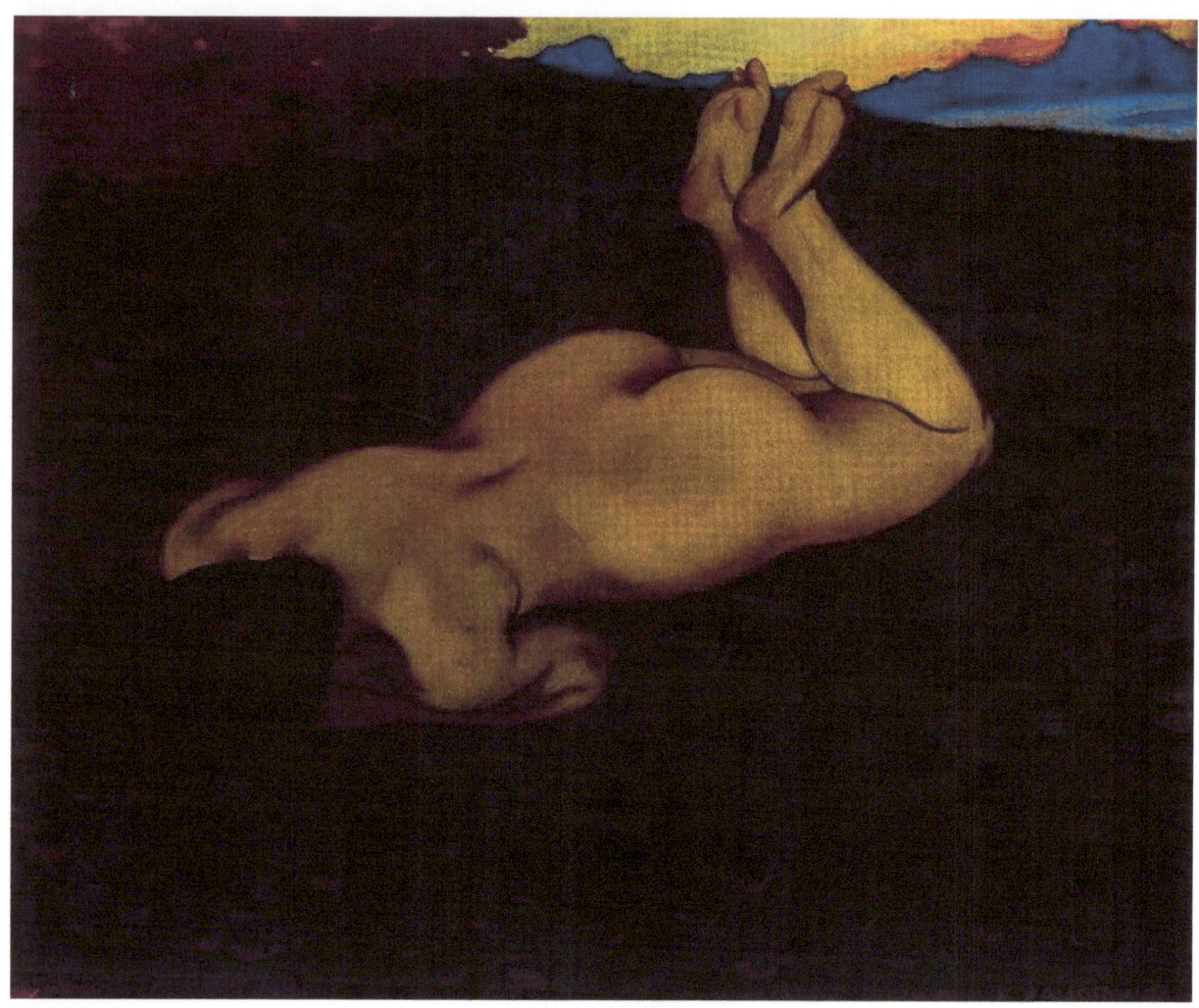

The Source, 1897, Magic Realism

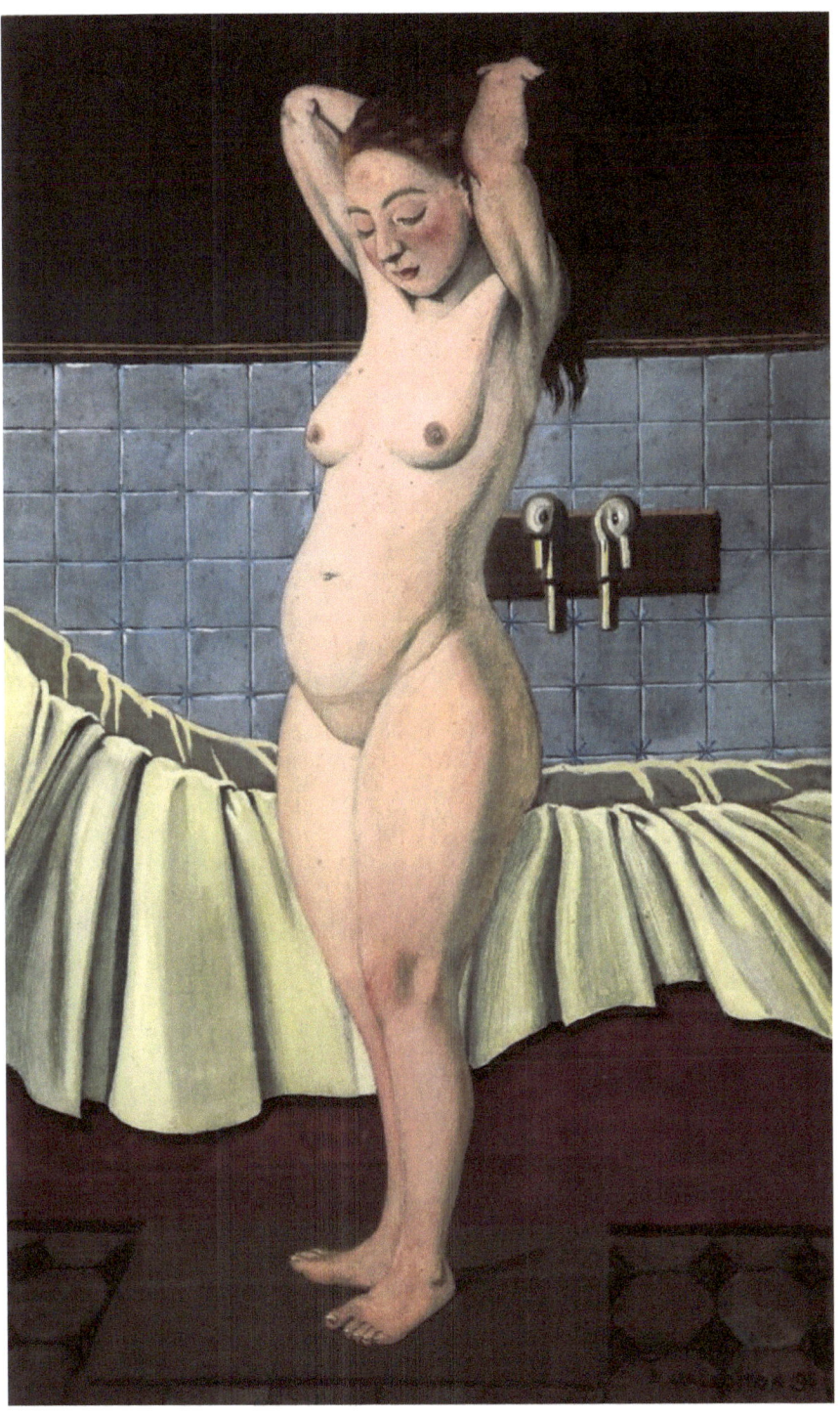

Woman aiu being capped Bath, 1897, Magic Realism

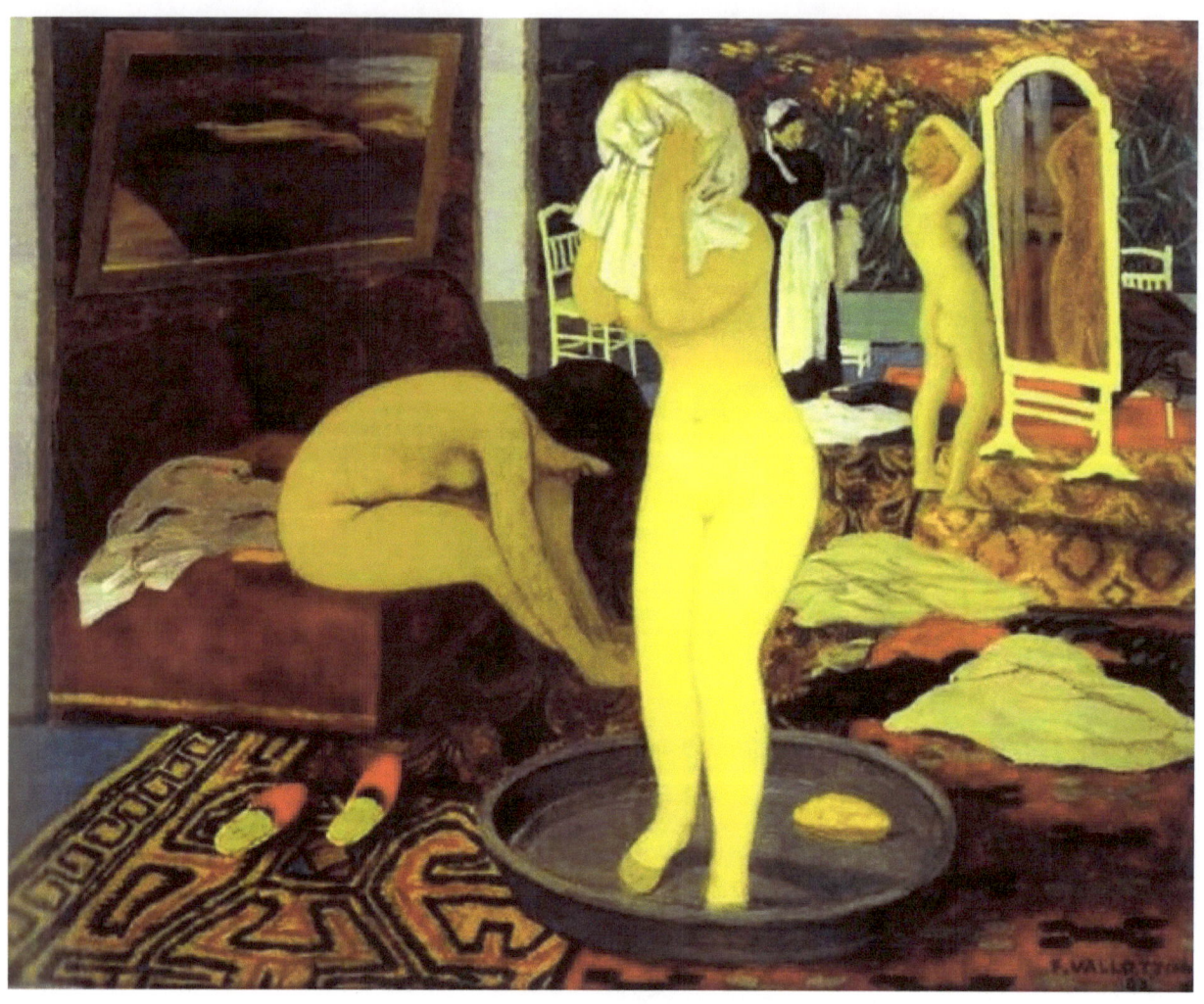

Women at Their Toilet Femmes leur toilette, 1897, Cloisonnism

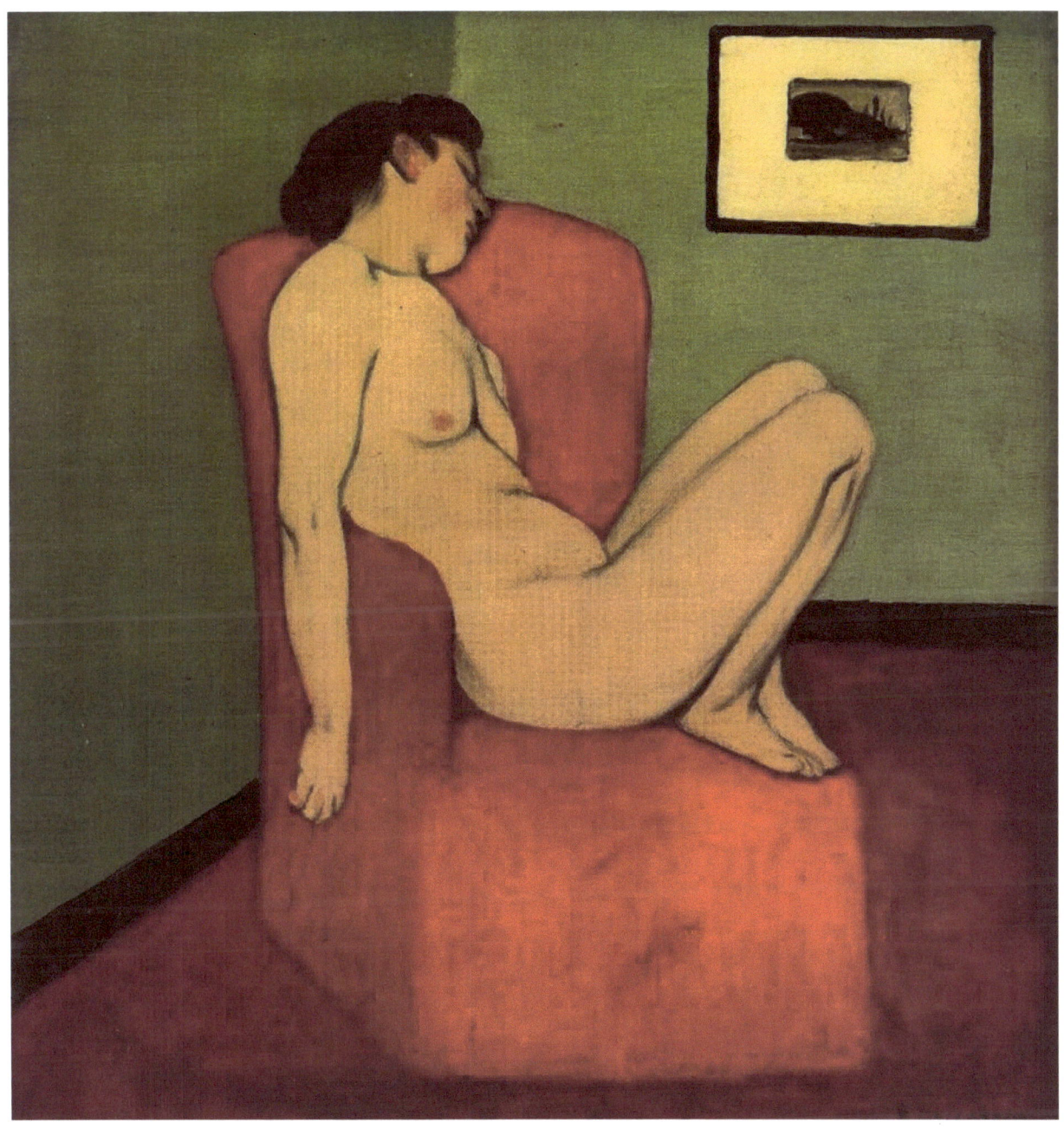

Seated Female Nude, 1897, Cloisonnism

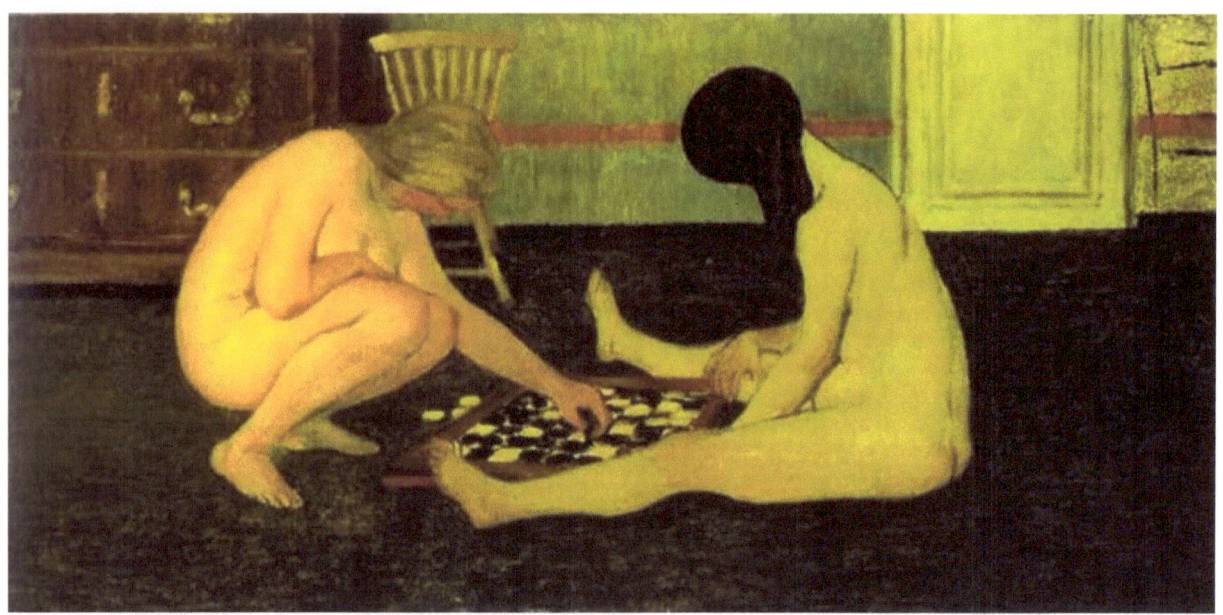

Naked Women Playing Checkers, 1897, Cloisonnism

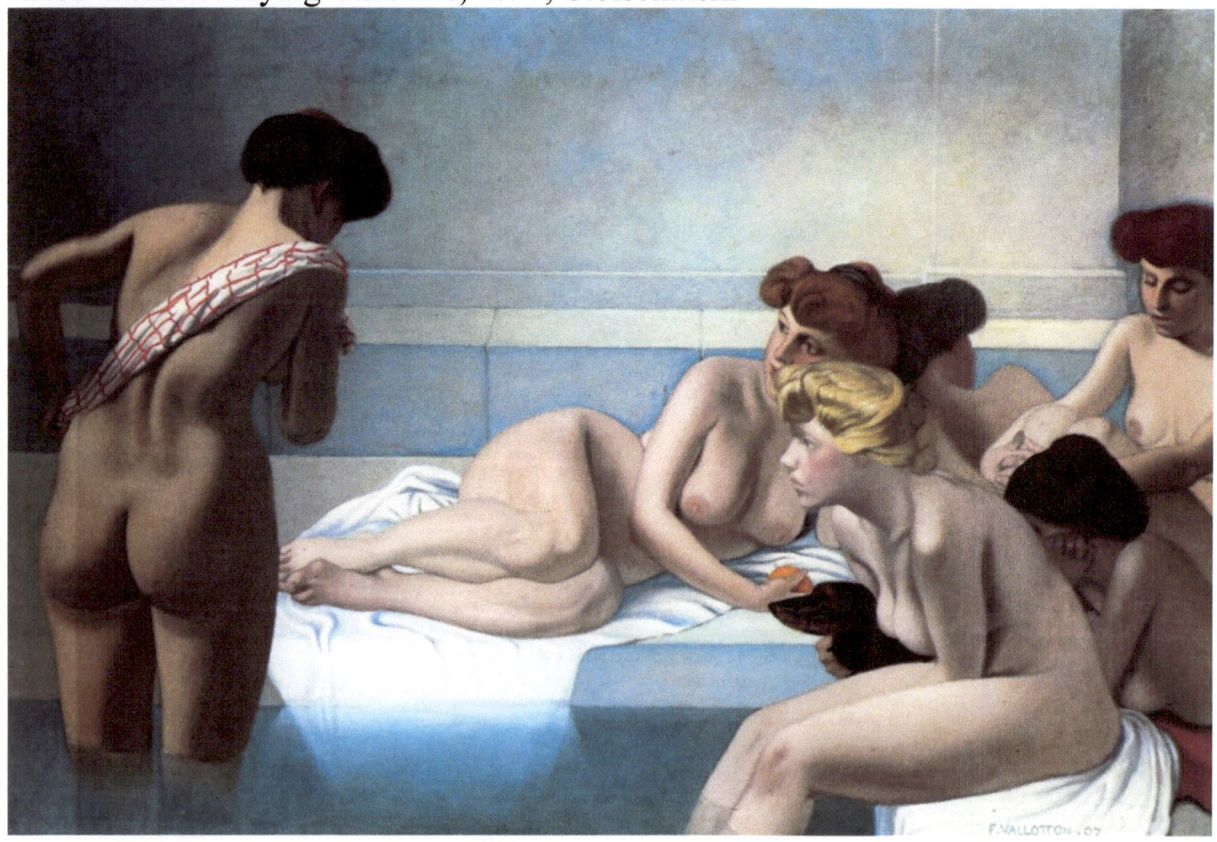

The Turkish bath, 1907, Magic Realism

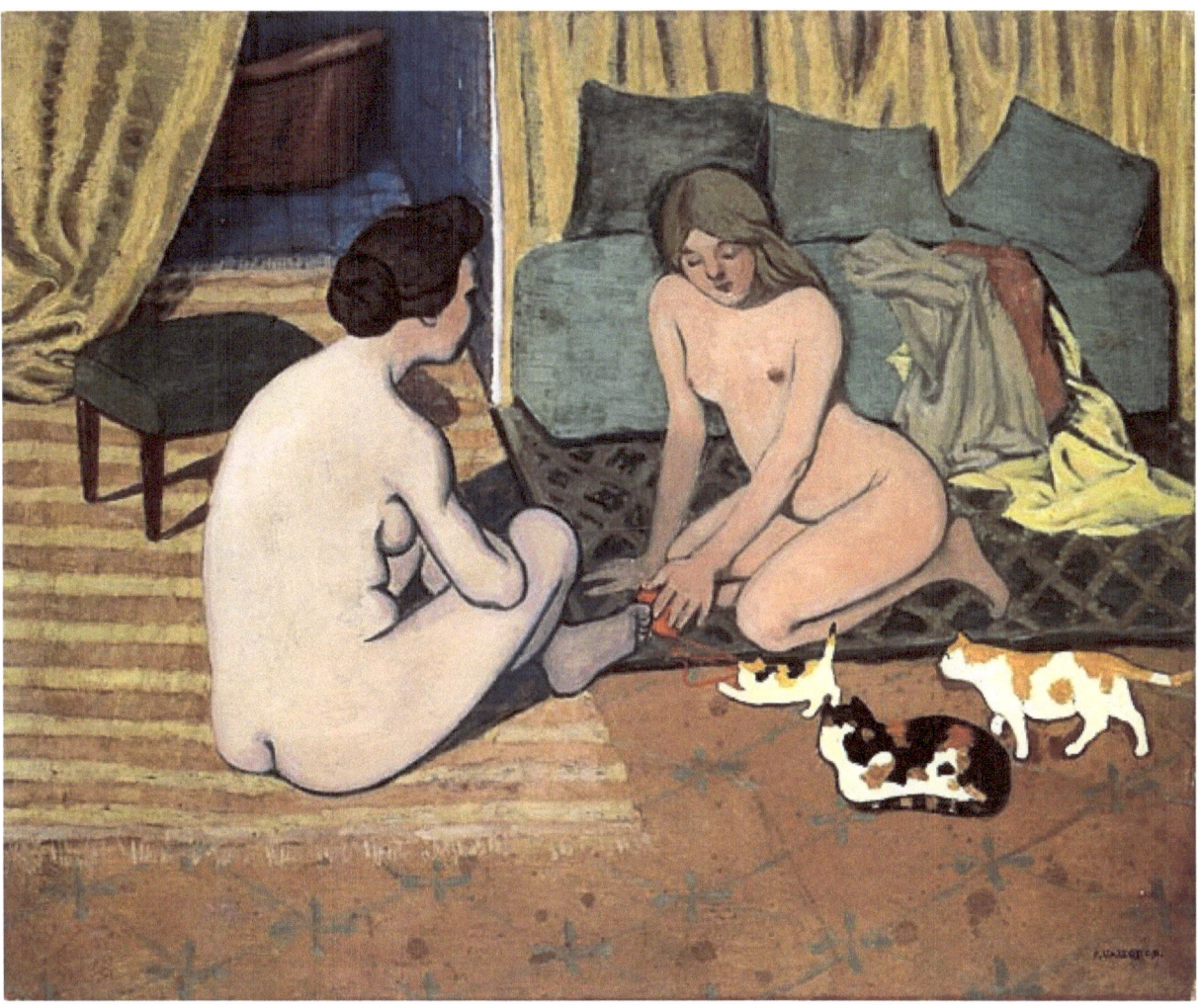

Naked women to cats, 1898, Cloisonnism

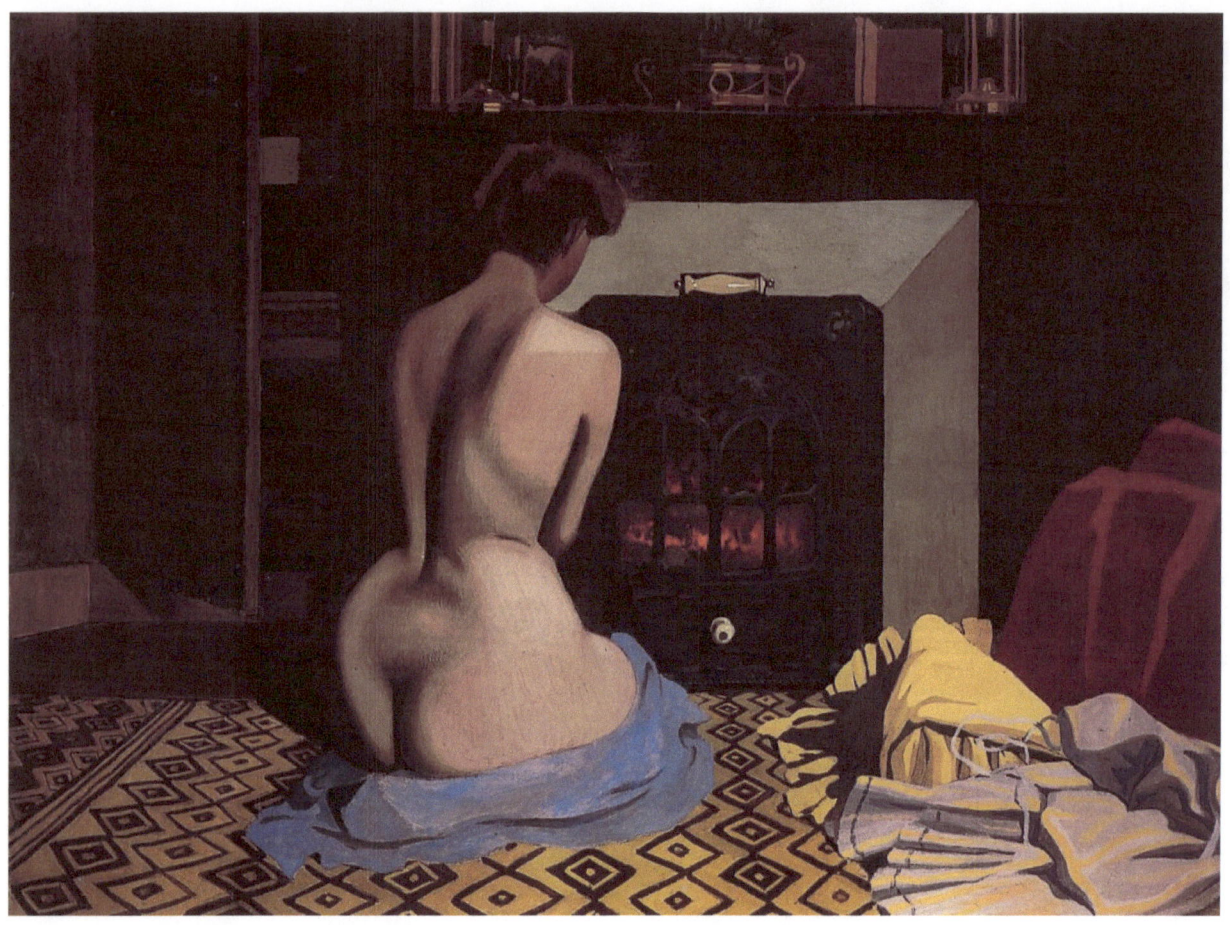

Nude at the Stove, 1900, Post-Impressionism

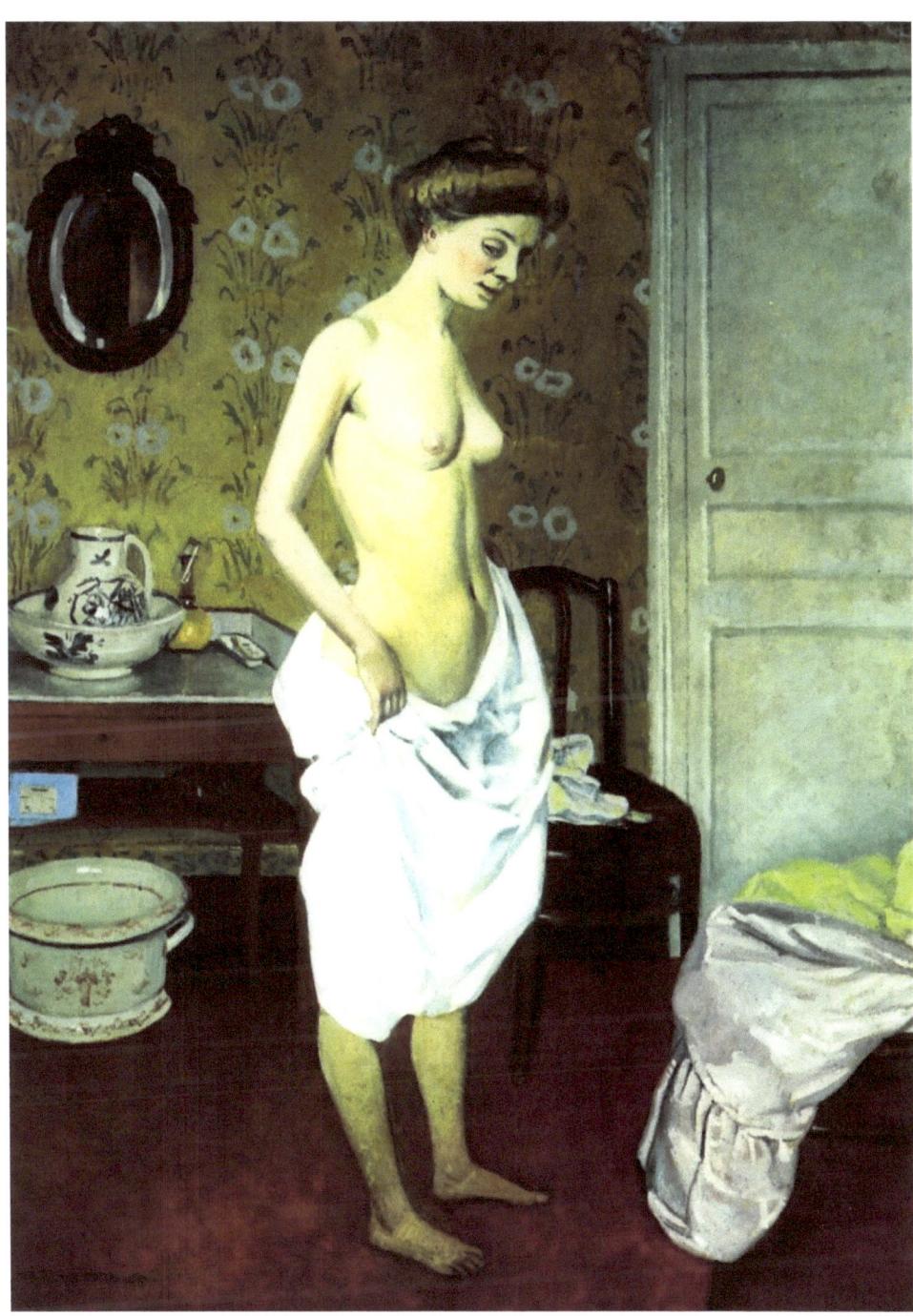

The Toilet, 1905, Magic Realism,

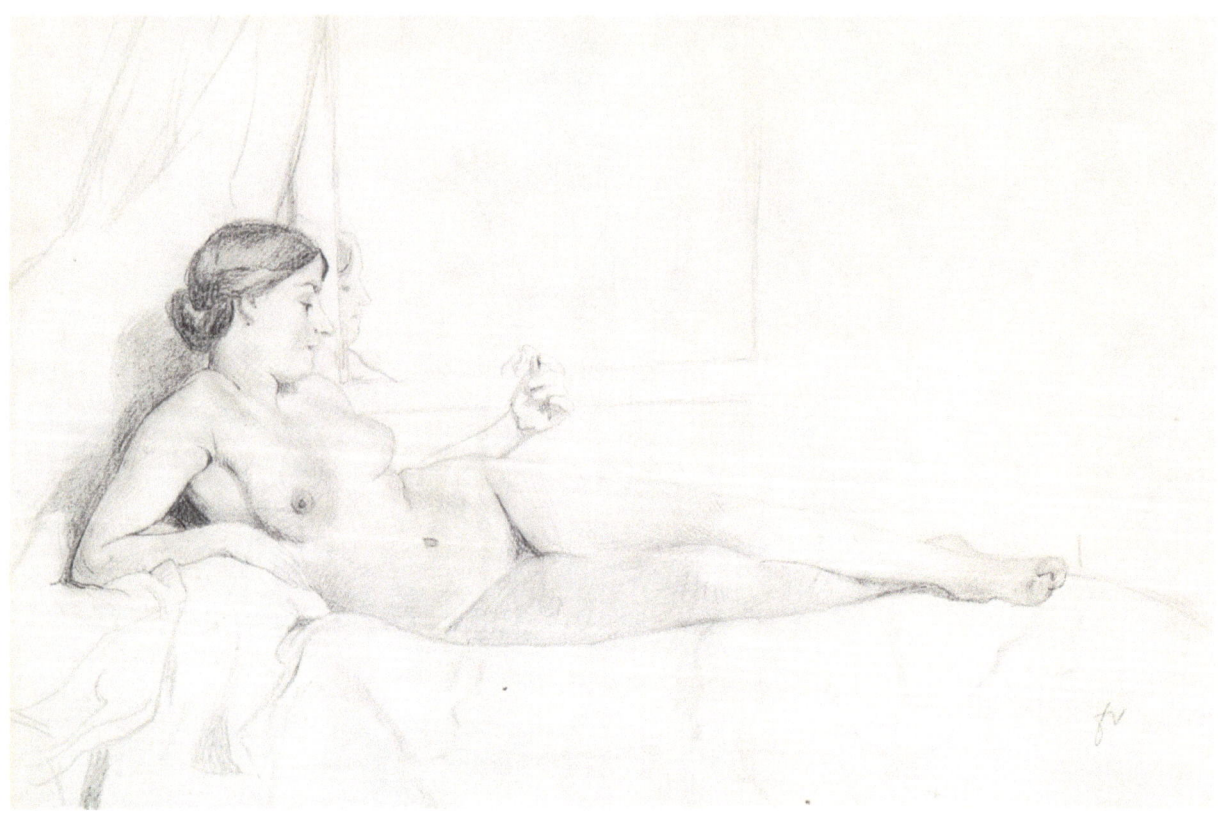

Reclining Nude on a couch, 1905, Realism

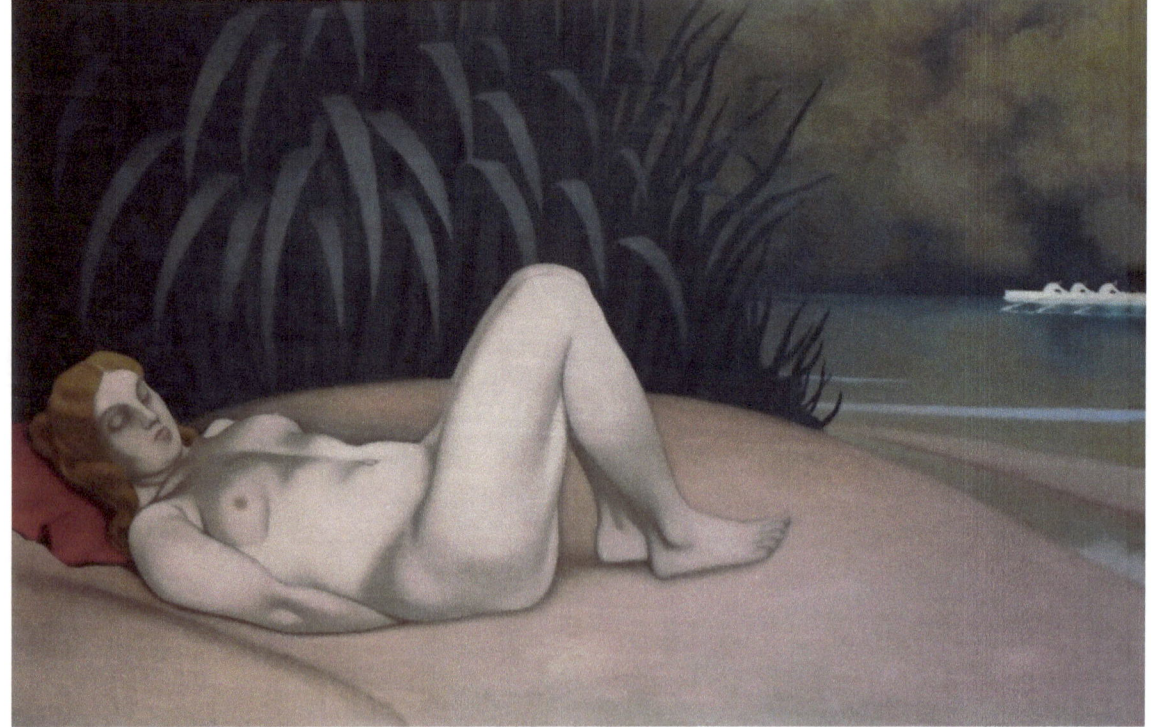

Naked woman sleeping at the edge of the water, 1921, Magic Realism,

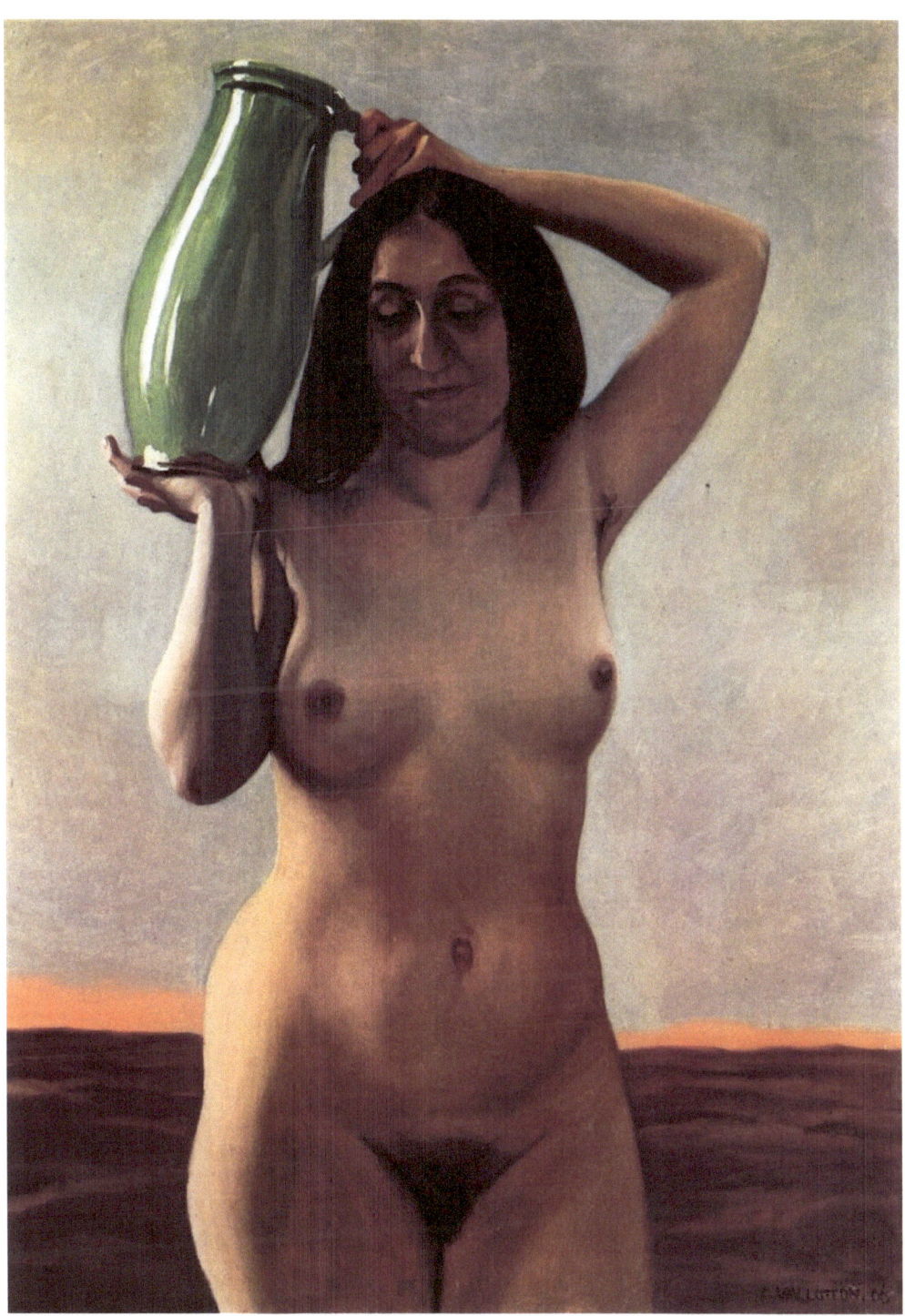

Woman with the Jug, 1906, Magic Realism

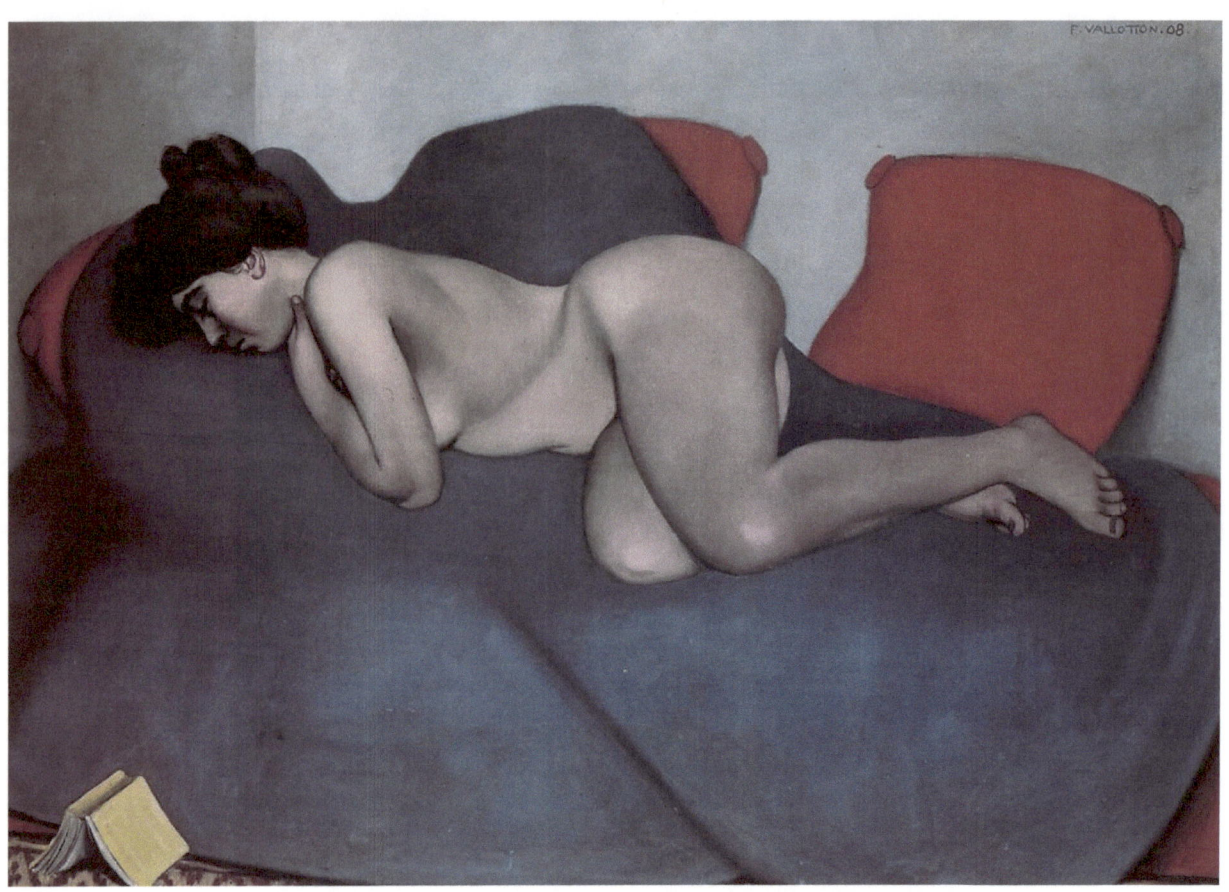

Sleep 1908, Magic Realism

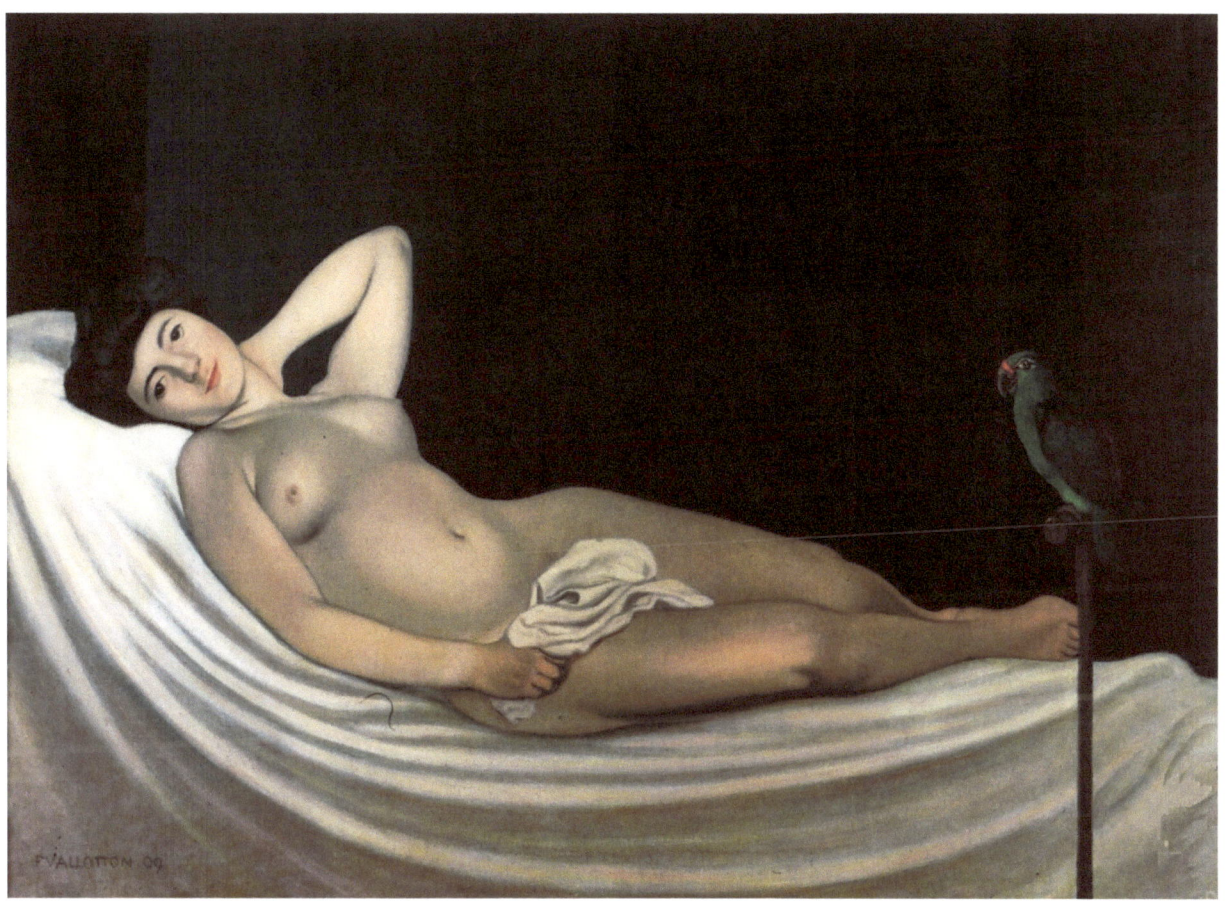

The Woman with the Parrot, 1909, Magic Realism

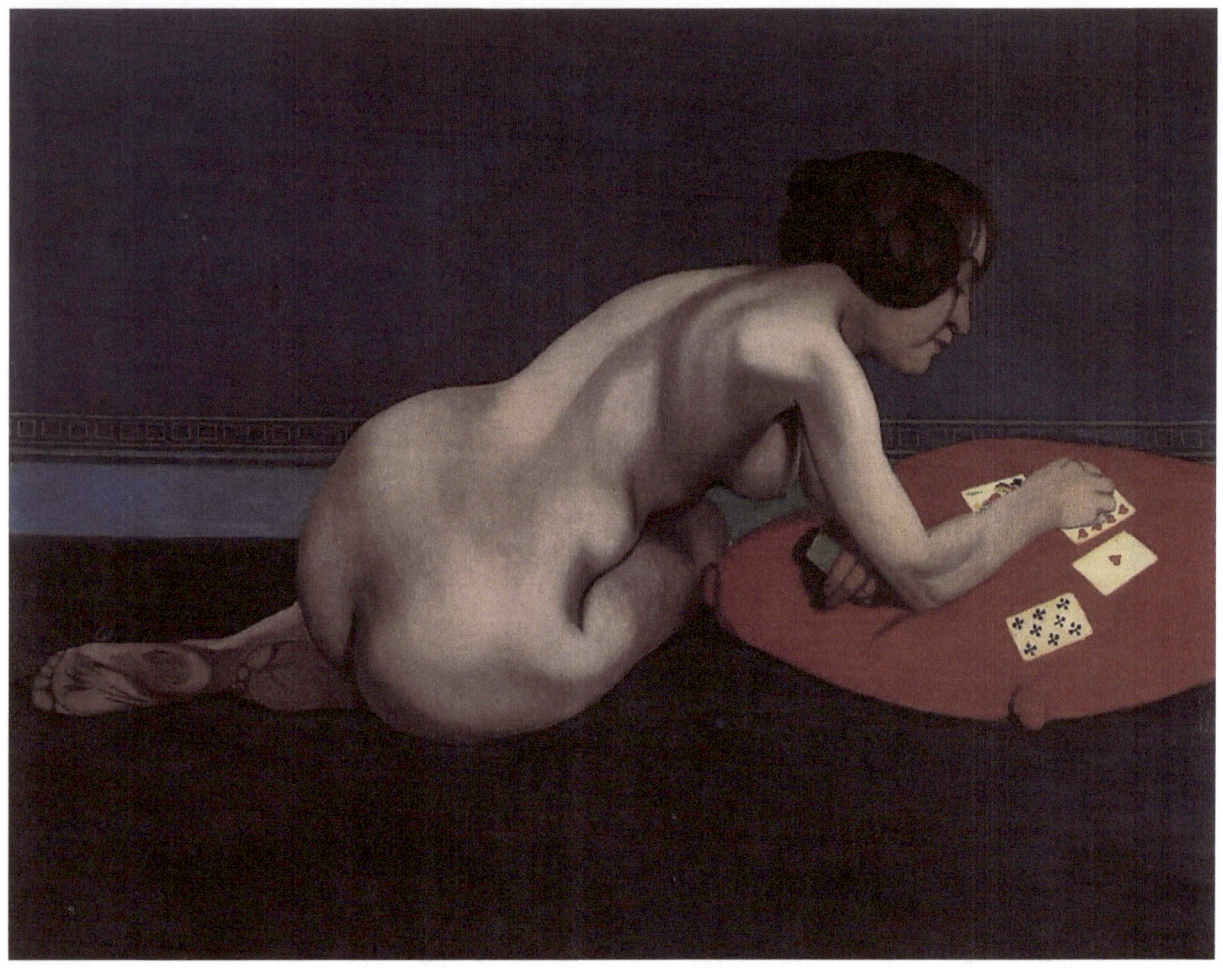

Solitaire (also known as Nude Playing Cards), 1912, Magic Realism

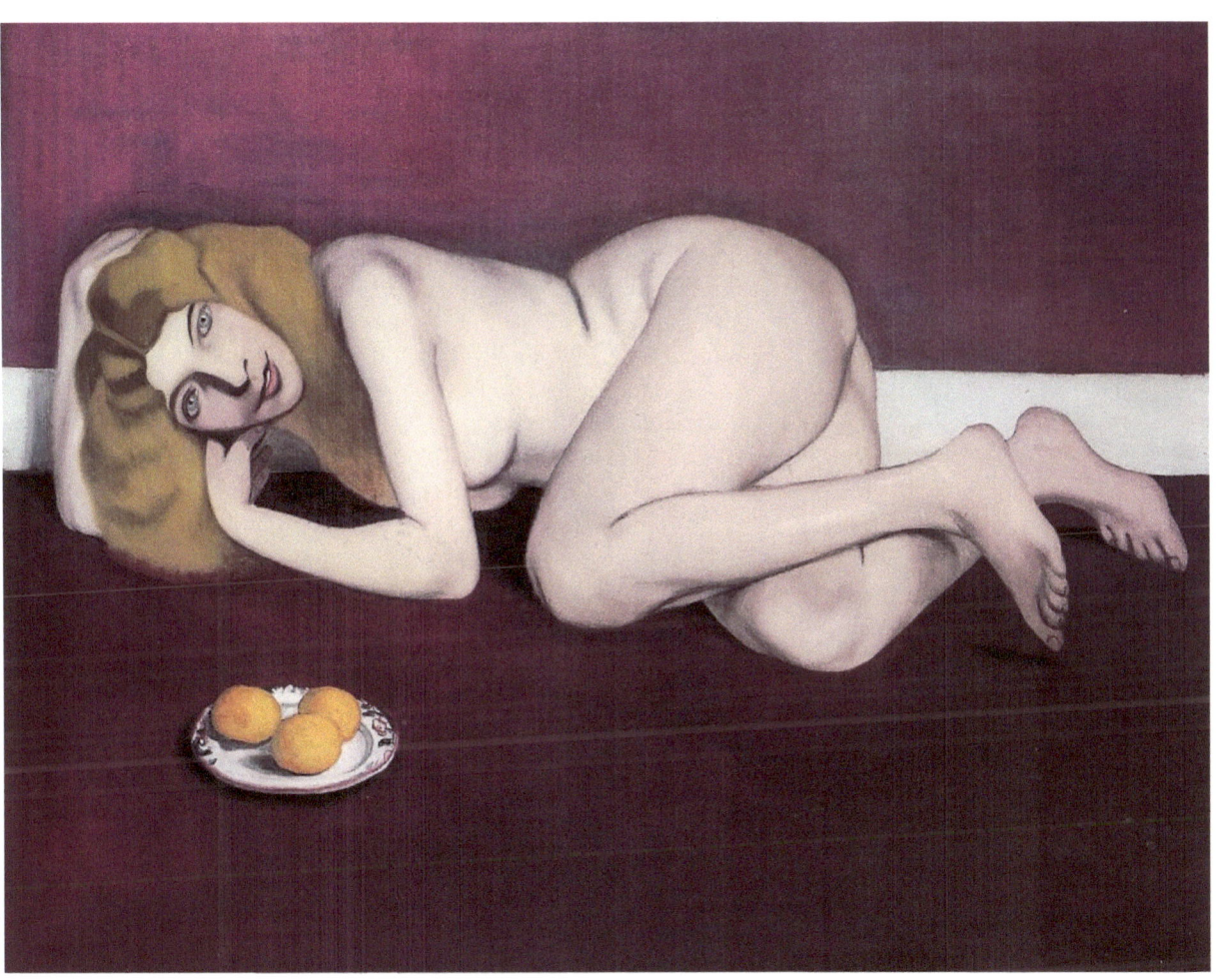

Nude Blond Woman with Tangerines, 1913, Magic Realism

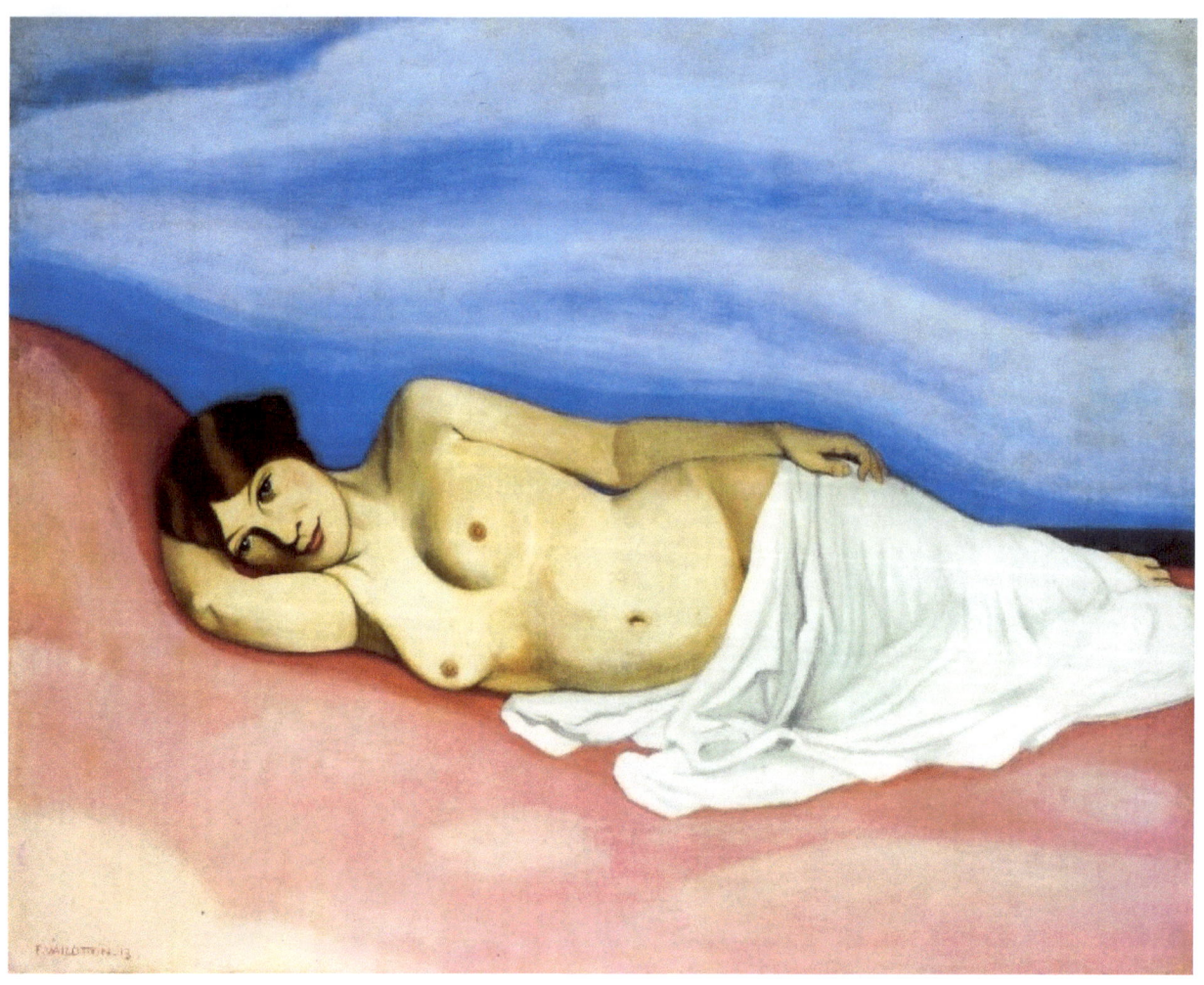

Nude in Bed, 1913, Magic Realism

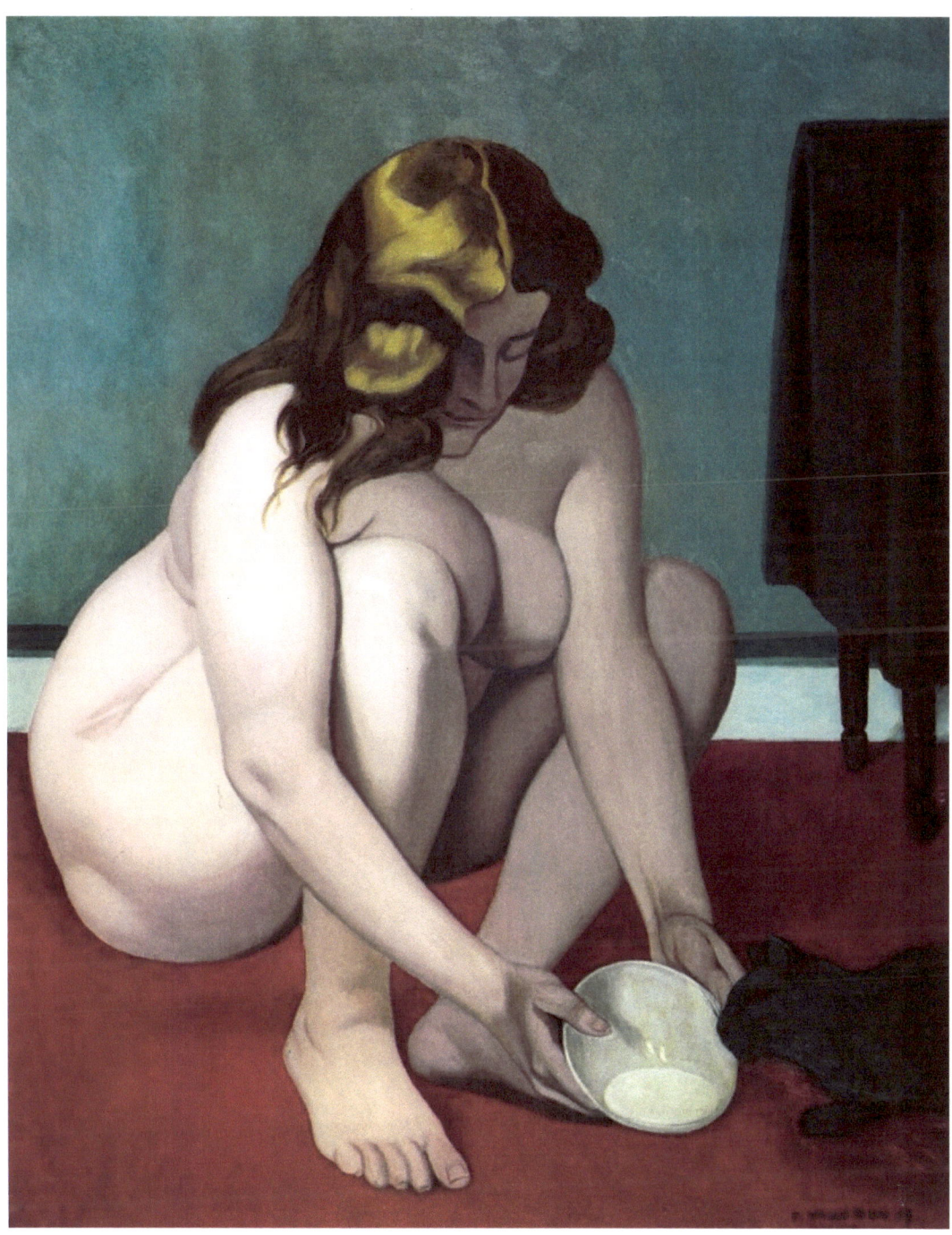

Squatted woman offering of milk to a cat, 1919, Magic Realism

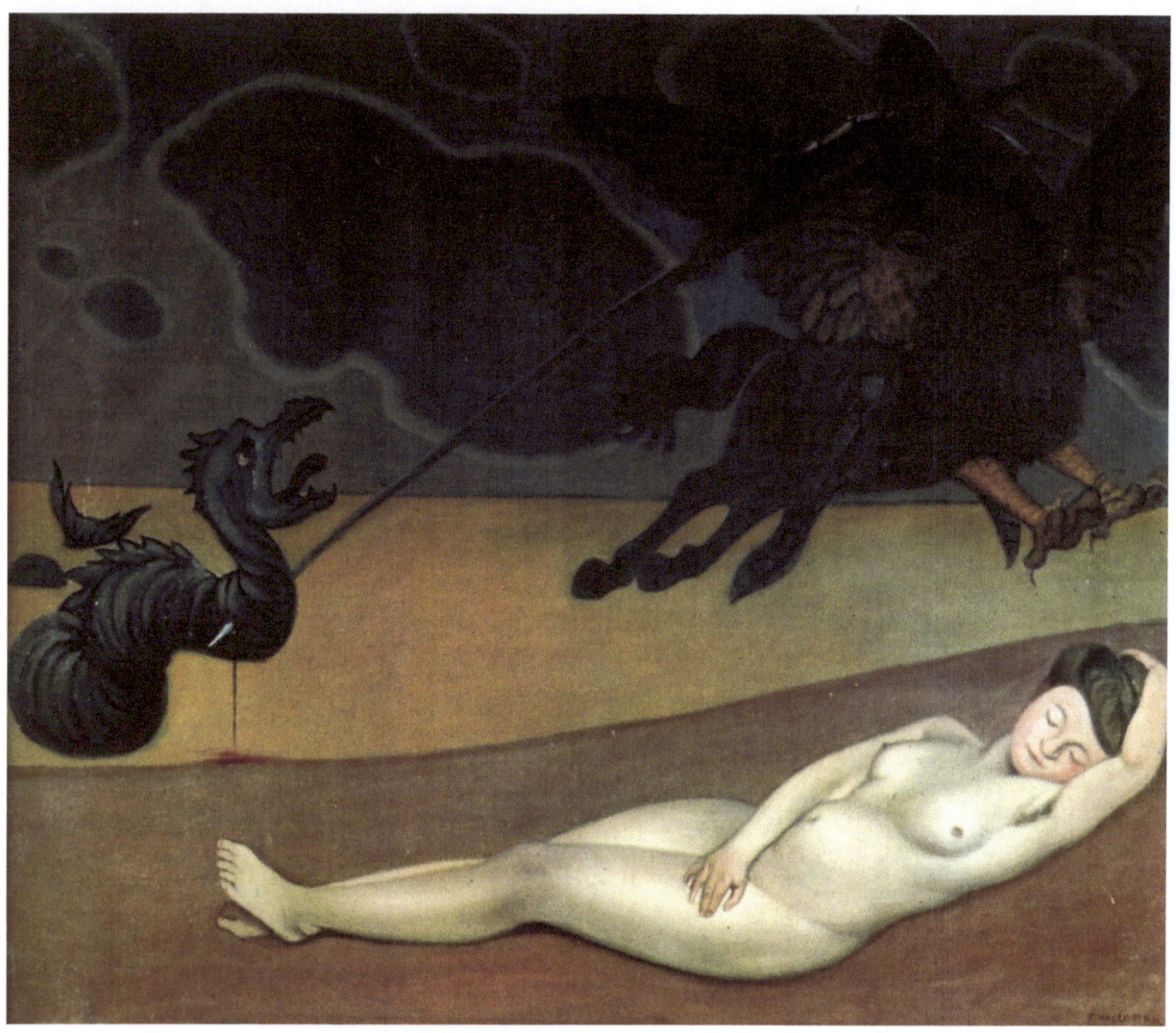

Roger delivering Angelica, 1907, Magic Realism

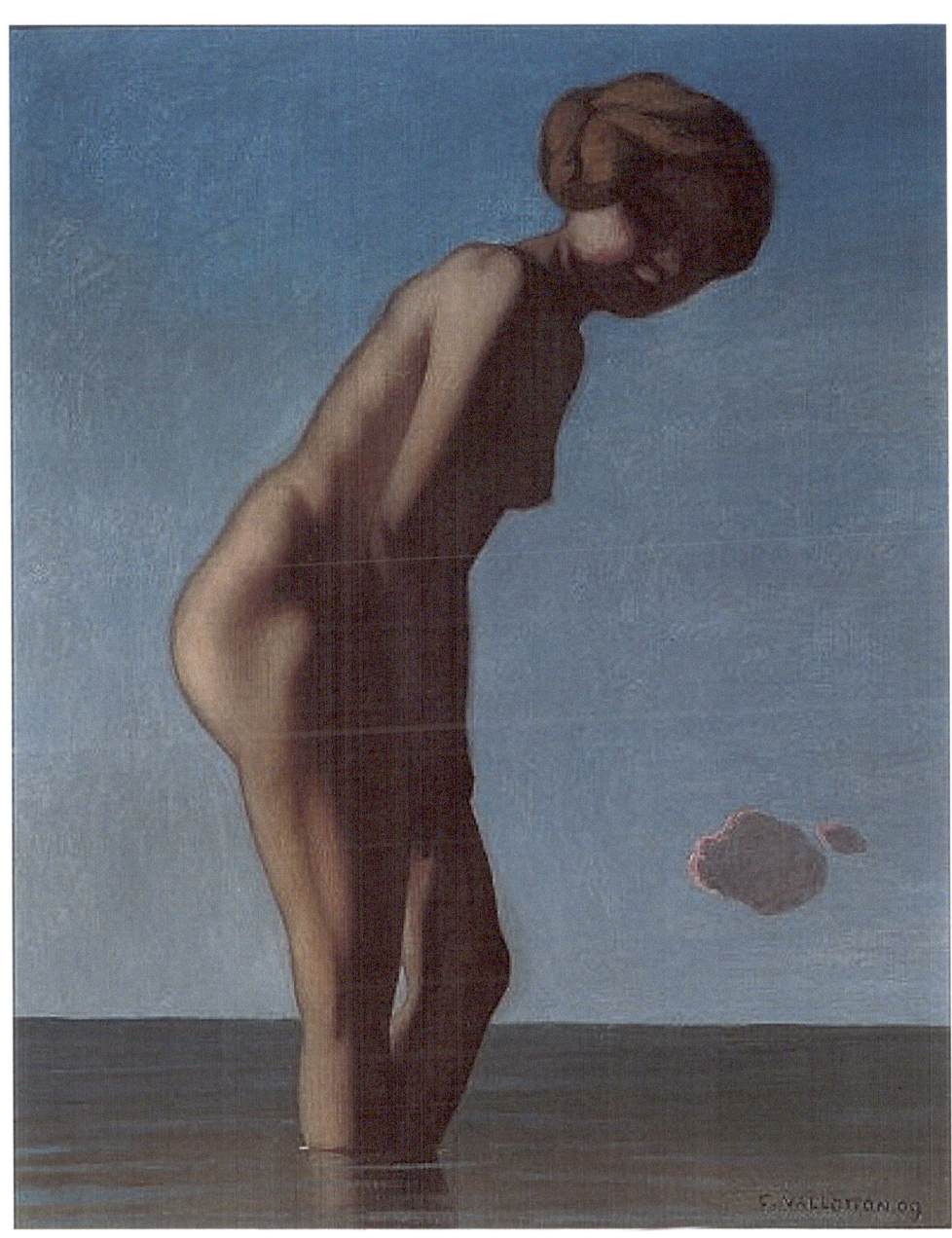

Bather looked to the right, 1909, Magic Realism

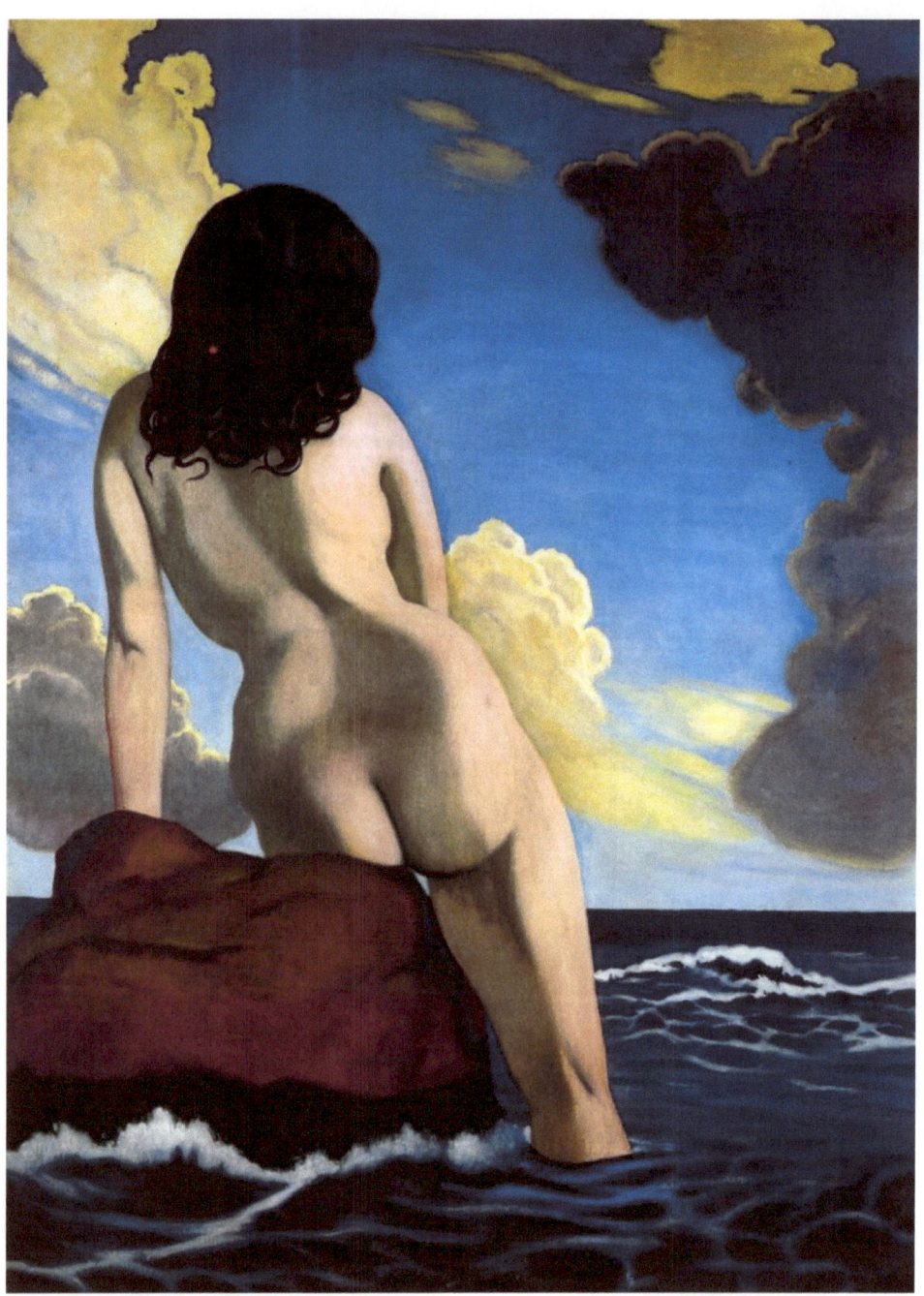

Bather, stormy sky, 1916, Magic Realism

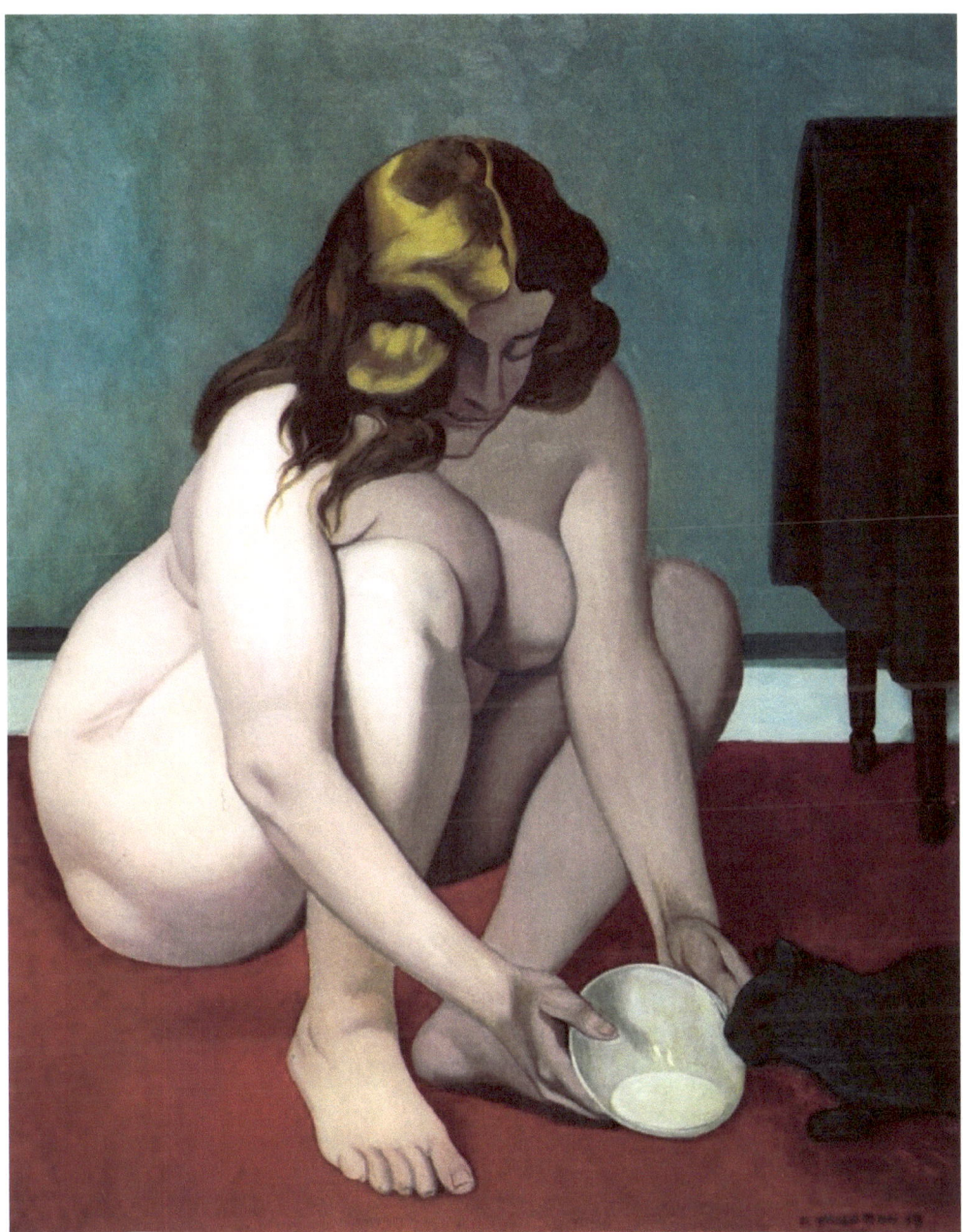

Squatted woman offering of milk to a cat, 1919, Magic Realism